A Bridge

From the UK

Matthew Woodward

LANNA HALL PUBLISHING

A LANNA HALL BOOK

First published in Great Britain in 2018
by Lanna Hall Publishing

Copyright © 2018 Matthew Woodward

ISBN 978-1-52170-767-8

Cover design by Colin Brooks
Illustrations by Mark Hudson
Edited by Caroline Petherick

www.matthew-woodward.com

'The passion for trains and railways is, I have been told, incurable.'

Eric Lomax, *The Railway Man*

Contents

Introduction

The United States space programme did not attempt to land Neil Armstrong and Buzz Aldrin on the moon with their very first Apollo rocket. Instead each mission grew in complexity from the previous one. My journey to Singapore was built upon the experiences of a previous trip from Edinburgh to Shanghai. I wrote about this and life on the rails in Russia and Mongolia in my first book, *Trans-Siberian Adventures*. This was the story of my escape from the office and my first steps towards becoming a rail adventurer.

Almost any person with some organisational skills, a sense of adventure and enough time on their side could decide to undertake a journey like this one. The great thing is that you don't need to wield an ice axe or to be fitter than an ultra-marathon runner to have a rail-based adventure; just a sense of humour, an interest in the world, and if possible a means to make reasonable coffee along the way.

I lost count of how many bridges I crossed, but I have featured some of the more significant ones that I went over or passed by on my journey south. They were the tangible markers of my progress towards Singapore. But more than that, their role in modern history and cinema was the inspiration for this book. A journey that connected *A Bridge Too Far* with *The Bridge on the River Kwai* was an irresistible idea.

Rail timetables are constantly changing, sometimes for the better, sometimes for the worse. A few of the trains I used are no longer operating, and others have taken their place, but with differences to their exact route and timetable. Whilst Europe seeks ever faster daytime intercity services to compete with airlines, the long-distance night trains in Russia and much of Asia are fortunately still alive and well. In fact, new investment may soon offer the prospect of new routes to travel south through Laos and Cambodia and into Thailand.

Many of the place names in this book are translated into English from a variety of languages; the spellings I have used are the most common ones and usually those that appeared in published train timetables at the time of my journey.

If you seek inspiration for your next adventure, but are not sure yet if you want to become a polar explorer or a deep-sea diver, then I would simply quote Sir Ran Fiennes: 'Anything is an adventure if you stop doing what you normally do.' Whatever your journey might be, live dangerously – and do it before someone talks you out of it.

Matthew Woodward
Chichester, West Sussex, 2018

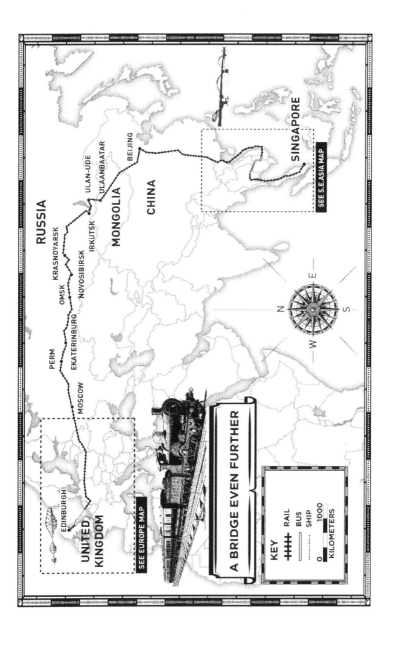

RUSSIA

EDINBURGH
UNITED
KINGDOM

SEE EUROPE MAP

MOSCOW
PERM
EKATERINBURG
OMSK
NOVOSIBIRSK
KRASNOYARSK
IRKUTSK
ULAN-UDE
ULAANBAATAR

MONGOLIA

BEIJING

CHINA

SINGAPORE

SEE S.EASIA MAP

N
W — E
S

A BRIDGE EVEN FURTHER

KEY
+++++ RAIL
BUS
········· SHIP

0   1000
KILOMETERS

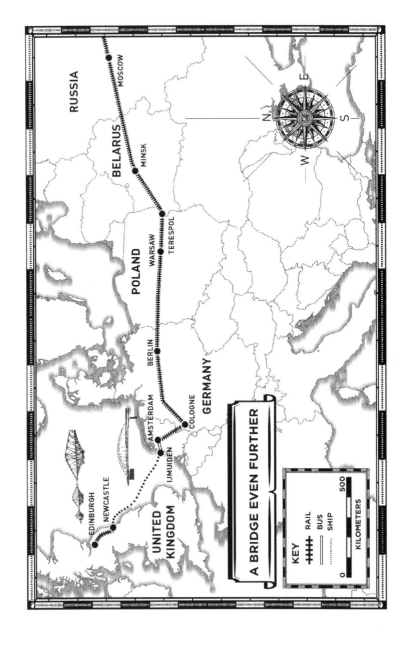

A BRIDGE EVEN FURTHER

KEY
RAIL
BUS
SHIP

KILOMETERS
0   500

RUSSIA
MOSCOW
BELARUS
MINSK
POLAND
WARSAW
TERESPOL
BERLIN
GERMANY
AMSTERDAM
COLOGNE
IJMUIDEN
NEWCASTLE
EDINBURGH
UNITED
KINGDOM

N
W
S
E

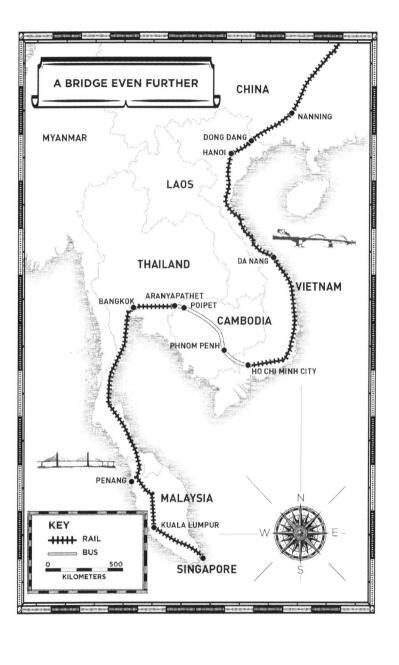

A BRIDGE EVEN FURTHER

CHINA

NANNING

MYANMAR

DONG DANG
HANOI

LAOS

THAILAND

DA NANG

VIETNAM

BANGKOK   ARANYAPATHET
POIPET
CAMBODIA

PHNOM PENH

HO CHI MINH CITY

PENANG

MALAYSIA

KUALA LUMPUR

SINGAPORE

KEY
+H+H RAIL
BUS
0   500
KILOMETERS

N
W   E
S

One: Colonel Bogey

Thailand, January 2008

The third-class carriage on the train from Nam Tok to Thornburi was completely full. Not in an Indian commuter train sense, with people sitting on the roof, but rather that there was nowhere left to sit or stand in the shade inside the carriage. The passengers were a mixture of locals coming back from countryside markets and backpackers returning from the infamous Bridge on the River Kwai.

I must have been sitting on the wrong side of the carriage, as I could soon feel the sun burning the back of my neck. The locals always know which side to sit on; they even seem to avoid the indirect radiation of daylight where possible, let alone the power of direct sunshine on their skin. Coughing as politely as possible, I was ingesting a potent mixture of dust, diesel smoke and ash blown in through the open window as we chugged down the line in the direction of Bangkok. I love open windows on trains. Not just for the welcome breeze on a steaming hot day, but also for the way it allows you to directly sample the smells, the sounds and atmosphere of the world right

7

outside. If you dared, you could touch a lot of what was going on without even getting out of your seat. Every now and again a single rotating ceiling fan delivered a waft of cool air in my direction, but it was an all too short-lived relief from the heat. Sitting on a sticky green plastic bench seat, I was surrounded by a group of kids I assumed to be students. They wore city clothes and took endless pictures of each other with the latest mobile phones available in Thailand.

Monks chanted prayers on the passing platforms, mobile vendors shouted out what they were selling as they moved up and down the train, and at each stop passengers bundled on, looking optimistically for somewhere to sit. In the corridor at the end of the carriage behind me was a man dressed in a dark military uniform. He wore aviator shades and sported a nickel-plated pistol on his right hip. I would guess from growing up watching films like *Dirty Harry* that it was a .357 magnum, but with a shorter barrel than the one Clint Eastwood favoured. It was a very old-school choice of gun, and a bit scary to think that if he were to fire such a weapon, the bullet would probably pass through both ends of the train and everything in between.

As we pulled out of the short stop at Kanchanaburi I could hear the guard at the end of our carriage asking to see tickets. His battle cry was '*Khaw do tua, krab; Khaw do tua, krab,*' but he occasionally spoke in English too – just as well, given the number of *farangs* (foreigners) on board who spoke no Thai, or at least no Thai that a Thai person would understand. I count myself amongst those, as I can only speak bar Thai. I have a friend who only speaks golf Thai and another who speaks just spa Thai. If you are only going to learn a few words, you might as well make every one of them count in your lifestyle.

As the guard drew level with my seat I caught my first glimpse of him. He was a fit man in his thirties wearing a paramilitary uniform, cut in a very Thai way – a cut that would be impossible to wear with even the slightest love of beer. He wore a few badges, some medals, and what looked like parachute wings on his chest. Were he not the conductor of a train, I would probably have mistaken him for a warrant officer in the parachute regiment. Glancing at me briefly he just said, 'Ticket,' and waited whilst I rummaged around in my bag.

My little white and green Thai rail ticket was crumpled and a bit grubby, but only a few hours old. I had purchased it even before the sun rose in Bangkok that morning. Handing it over, he studied it, and looked at me a bit harder as if working out what to do. 'No ticket,' he said. I pointed at the thing in his hand and reaffirmed my belief that it was in fact a ticket. 'No ticket,' he said. 'One way.' Had I known this I would have been feeling desperately guilty, but I had no time for such an emotion. I thought that my ticket had been good value at just 100 baht, and this explained why. That was six hours on the train for less than £2. But the full return fare was actually £4.

Feeling rather embarrassed I waited to hear of my

fate. The students put down their phones and looked on with growing interest. The carriage seemed a little quieter now. The Thai women opposite who had been chatting incessantly were silent. I didn't look round, but I also considered if Dirty Harry might now have his hand on his hip, limbering his fingers, in case I was the punk who was going to make his day. But did I feel lucky? How would this foolish foreigner, who might even be a fare dodger, be dealt with? A fine perhaps? Thrown off the train? Escorted to Kanchanaburi police station? Detention and deportation? My mind ran away with possible outcomes whilst he proceeded to get out a large brown notebook. This didn't look good. I thought about a bribe, but didn't see how this was going to be possible with so many people now watching us. Once he starts writing, I thought, there will be no going back.

I smiled at him and shrugged my shoulders in a way to look as passive and helpless as possible. I had often noticed the Thai preoccupation with saving face and avoiding direct confrontation. This didn't seem to make much difference today, though, as he quickly got to work on his paperwork whilst resting his heavy pad on the seat next to me. After a few minutes of careful scribbling he produced a stamp from his satchel (a kind of Thai Railways issue man bag) and franked the form, as if to make my fate official.

It turned out not to be an arrest warrant or even a court summons, but a special kind of ticket for people who had no ticket. I didn't have long to wait to find out how much this piece of paper was going to cost, as he tore the white copy from his pad and handed it to me whilst filing the yellow copy in his book. 'You have ticket now. You pay 100 baht.' That was the same cost as if I had bought it at the station. Smiles all round – thanking him as best as I knew how for such an unforeseen situation: '*Khorb khun mark na krub.*' I even offered a mini *wai* (the Thai polite bow), which he seemed to appreciate (or perhaps it was so bad that he just found it funny). Daring to raise my eyes now and look around at my fellow passengers, I wished that I also knew the Thai for 'nothing to see here – I have a ticket'.

With that bit of excitement over, I zoned out of the renewed din of the carriage and reflected on my day. I had spent the morning at the Commonwealth war graves at Kanchanaburi before inspecting the modern bridge over the River Kwae. Everything was absolutely immaculate at the cemetery. I had never considered before how the state of the graves would lift my spirits, but the devotion to neatness seemed wholly respectful and appropriate, and somehow made me feel much more positive than perhaps I otherwise would have been. As a repressed Englishman it took me some effort not to get too misty-eyed as I laid a Lady Haig cross on the memorial that I had inscribed with my failing hotel ballpoint pen, 'To the Railway Men'.

Back at the station, I found a *songthaew* (a van used as a share taxi) with its driver sleeping in the cab, and encouraged him with a few banknotes to take me along to the bridge. We set off, then after 10 minutes he knocked on the panel behind the cab, the signal for me to jump off, and waved manically at me as he sped off to find somewhere else to finish his lunchtime kip. I must have paid him far too much.

The street was swarming with frenzied Asian tourists buying t-shirts and souvenirs in the fashion of a closing down sale. I wasn't at all sure that they even understood what the Death Railway was. I had to escape from this, so I headed upriver on foot. After a few hundred yards I found a little restaurant on the river bank, where I could observe the bridge and gather my thoughts with a little more peace and tranquillity.

A man appeared from nowhere and before long I was enjoying a cold Chang beer and some fried rice, with only the occasional speedboat and an angry squawking bird to disturb me. I tried to connect my world today to this place 60 years before. Like many, my main reference point was David Lean's epic 1957 war film, which was actually shot in Sri Lanka. If you have seen the film you might remember the scene where Lieutenant Colonel Nicholson (Sir Alec Guinness) spots the wire where explosives have been planted on the bridge and comes down to the river bank with Colonel Saito to investigate its origin. I decided that my lunchtime location was pretty much identical to where Lieutenant Joyce had been hiding behind a rock with the detonator. Today there are no wires visible, and the train approaching from the direction of Hellfire Pass carries happy tourists rather than

Imperial Japanese Army dignitaries.

The bridge over the Kwae today isn't the same as the wooden one portrayed in the film, which was further upriver, before Allied bombs destroyed it. But somehow it still satisfied me to think that it was the bridge. At least it was Japanese-built, and parts of it dated back to 1944. The river was actually renamed Khwae Yai in the 1960s, to tie in with the success of the film. Despite this minor adjustment to history, what is very real are the graves of the 6,982 POWs buried a couple of miles away at the Kanchanaburi cemetery.

Back on the train I realised that I had been dozing off. I was coated in a fine brown dust and my throat was dry. We were about an hour behind schedule and the sun was beginning to set over Bangkok. The light is amazing at this time of the day and everything looks more moody and atmospheric. Getting off at Thornburi station, I brushed the dirt off as best as I could and bought a bottle of warm Coke from a street seller to lubricate my throat as I walked towards the river to find a boat to take me back to my hotel in Bang Rak. I nearly made it back without any further drama, but made the elementary mistake of standing on the stern of the ferry and getting soaked by the wash from a passing barge. Even the locals don't rate the water quality of the Chao Phraya river, and cower inside until the last possible moment when the boatman whistles that he is about to hit the pier, and it's time to make a jump for it.

Diving in the crystal-clear blue waters of the

Andaman Sea later that week, I found that the Bridge on the River Kwai seemed to regularly drift in and out of my thoughts. Perhaps I had some unfinished bridge business.

Two: The Railway Man

Edinburgh, July 2013

The Sheriff's Court in Edinburgh is a busy modern building behind the historic facade on the Royal Mile. I'm with bunch of potential jurors waiting to see who will be drawn out of the hat for jury service. Most of us make small talk, but a few braver souls approach the clerk with carefully rehearsed reasons to be excused. The case hasn't been called yet, and there is a constant stream of solicitors and advocates approaching a judge at the other end of the room. To begin with, I find myself trying to follow what is going on. It is all too easy to forget where I am and imagine that I'm watching a live version of a classic episode of a criminal drama on television. But this is real, and I start to feel uncomfortable about my intrusion into the lives of others. Trying to uncouple from all this, I get out a book that I have remembered to bring in case of a long wait. My second-hand copy of *The Railway Man* by Eric Lomax has lived a rough life, and its pages have folded corners and are yellow with age.

Eric Lomax was born in Edinburgh on 30th May 1919. From life as a post office clerk, he was commissioned in December 1940 as a second lieutenant in the Royal Signals and posted to Singapore. He became a prisoner of war in February 1942, and after a forced march to Changi Prison was transported to Kanchanaburi in Thailand, where with many thousands he was made to work on the infamous Burma railway. It wasn't until 1995 that the book of his experiences of the Death Railway and his life was finally published.

Transported to the River Kwai, I managed to escape the court and absorb myself in the brutality of Lomax's wartime world. The sounds of the jungle, the humidity, even the smell. But eventually the squawking in the trees turned out to be the clerk of the court asking for potential jurors to get ready for possible action. I put my book down just as the judge reappeared, and the clerk then began to call out names on pieces of paper drawn from his goldfish bowl. It crossed my mind as to if this was actually a goldfish bowl or a specialised legal object. Maybe the clerk of this court was just a keen fish keeper? I waited to hear my name called as those around me stood up one by one and shuffled past the accused over to the jury box. The fifteenth and final name was called, and a well-dressed business woman in my row joined the rest behind the jury bench.

The judge addressed those of us who were surplus to the court's requirements and thanked us for actually bothering to show up, before continuing with the case. I doubt that any case in court is going to be pleasant, but this one involved some pretty awful charges and was estimated to last several weeks. Whilst some people seem to thrive on doing their civic duty, I was frankly relieved not to be chosen. Blinking as I emerged in the bright light of a rare pleasant Edinburgh morning, my thoughts turned back to the River Kwai and I concluded two things. Firstly, that I needed to read more about Eric Lomax and the Burma railway, and secondly that maybe I could find some time to travel around Thailand and Myanmar by train.

When I had packed away my train travel bag after my first trip across Siberia I had no immediate plans to use it ever again. As is often the case with men and their hobbies, I seemed to have accumulated a lot of equipment over a short space of time. My train stuff now sat between my scuba gear and my yachting holdall in a quiet corner of a cupboard at home.

Returning from my first ever foray into long-range rail travel the previous year, there had been plenty of opportunities to tell my friends stories of my adventures on the Trans-Siberian railway. Reliving the experience was a reminder to me that I had probably crossed an imaginary line. I no longer needed to judge travel by how big the hotel room was. Instead I had a new series of metrics. How much did I laugh at the cock-ups? How many amazing people did I meet? How satisfying was it to overcome any problems along the way? I had now developed a taste for something different. I needed another adventure, and it needed to be overland. In short, I wanted once again to travel to somewhere implausible by train.

Becoming a long-range rail adventurer has no linear career path. I had a brief foray into climbing a few years before, and that was much more straightforward. You climbed a series of increasingly challenging summits that were graded by their difficulty. The climbing brochures were full of inspirational pictures and well packaged itineraries to maximise your chance of making it to the summit. You needed a climbing CV to prove that you might be suitable material for the peak you aspired to. Fancy a shot at Aconcagua? Have you climbed Kilimanjaro and Denali? If not, best do those first. However, for the rail adventurer there is no formal progression of trips, and there are just a few specialist brochures, mainly offering escorted tours to tourists with just a couple of weeks annual holiday and four or five star expectations.

My train CV contained a couple of student European Interrail trips, a journey part-way across Australia on the Indian Pacific, and of course my first ever Trans-Siberian trip to Shanghai. What was the next rung up the rail adventure ladder? I would be making this up as I went along.

I spent much time over the next few days re-reading nearly all the pages of the Man in Seat 61 website and imagining what it would be like to complete some of the grand journeys that it described. Mark Smith, who runs the site, has a habit of using comfortable-sounding words to make almost any route seem doable. It is part of the charm of Seat 61 that you can imagine the possibility of actually taking any journey that you dream of. The trick is to take positive action without delay, to anchor that possibility onto your own reality.

Looking at the possibilities, I certainly had a bit more confidence than when I had last considered a rail trip. I felt that I had since earned some of the boy scout badges in basic long-range rail survival. I made lots of notes in a newly acquired moleskin notebook and stuck brightly coloured post-it notes onto the large-scale 1956 National Geographic on the wall of my study. It would have been clever to have had a colour-based risk assessment of some of the routes – blue for crazy, purple for madness and orange for almost certain no return – but I didn't think of this at the time.

I had read about hardy travellers in the 1970s making the overland pilgrimage from the United Kingdom to Australia. Many of these journeys were completed by crossing Iran, Pakistan and India before heading onwards to Singapore to catch a ship down under. But with the Iranian Revolution and the Soviet invasion of Afghanistan came the end of what had become known as the hippie trail. At the time of writing it is actually still possible to cross by bus up through Nepal and into Tibet, but not by train. I quickly came to my own conclusion that the reality of my bumbling through the Hindu Kush solo was unrealistic. So, how else could I reach that far overland?

One afternoon the following week I went along to a client meeting with Mark Hudson, a friend who ran a marketing agency that I did some work for. It was an interesting way to earn a living. We'd been developing a promotional pitch for a drinks brand (think *The Fall and Rise of Reginald Perrin*), and a beer was needed after the lengthy presentation to clear our minds.

Our post-match discussions were about anything but the pitch. We chatted about one of our favourite subjects, war films. Mark was a keen amateur war historian with a particular passion for Operation Market Garden, the Allied attempt to capture the bridges across the Rhine in 1944. In the late noughties we had walked through the villages on the outskirts of Arnhem, following the route and the skirmishes of the Allied advance. Tonight we spent far too long discussing the accuracy of the 1977 blockbuster *A Bridge Too Far*. It would seem that Richard Attenborough had gone to considerable lengths to get exactly the right American armour into the film, but its German tanks were obviously Leopard 1's, a tank made about 20 years after the war. We concluded that this is nearly as big a crime as the electric doorbell appearing in a scene from *Battle of Britain*.

Thinking about this some more in my taxi back to the station, bridges were significant things in wars but they were also pretty vital to long-distance rail adventures. What if I could connect up these bridges by train? How far could I actually go?

The breakthrough moment was back in my study the following day. Looking again at the map, rather than try to cross the war-torn territories of the Middle East, there was actually a more practical solution. I could head from Edinburgh through eastern Europe and into Russia. From Siberia, and across the Gobi Desert to Beijing. From there I could just keep heading south, as for as the tracks would take me. Could I get as far as Singapore?

The following week I met Keith Parsons, my rail adventure mentor, to give him an update on my new plan over a curry so hot that I had a severe case of hiccups and couldn't speak for most of the meal. The problem that I have always found with curry is that it can become rather too competitive amongst friends. Someone orders a madras, the next person ups the stakes to a vindaloo, and then to remain in the game you really have to order something even more extreme. But like train travel, chilli is addictive and I crave the endorphins. Keith has a way of gently encouraging me to do things before I have realised that I'm going to do them myself. So I was expecting a string of detailed questions on my plan, but rather disarmingly he had just a single question for me: When was I planning to go? I thought about this for a moment, and high on a cocktail of endorphins and alcohol, I told him that I would like to go in December. Decision made; I had three months to formulate a plan.

I had been on the Trans-Mongolian train once before, so I would know the ropes for the first leg going east, but beyond Beijing I would have a more challenging time crossing countries with unconnected ticketing systems and some interesting frontiers as I headed south. The Chinese crossing into Vietnam at Da Dong was apparently not a friendly one. The Thai crossing into Malaysia involved a night in bandit country, and the biggest problem of all was Cambodia, with its lack of any modern railway, just a few wooden carts that were propelled along the rails by outboard motors.

My confidence in the plan progressively grew as I found agents and contacts in several countries along the route who seemed to understand what would be needed. I could see two ways of doing this journey. One way was to just turn up in each place and try to book tickets a day or two ahead; the other was to synchronise as much of the journey as possible and plan it in advance. A past life in crisis management led me on the more organised path. I felt better about getting as much as possible pre-arranged. The trip would be one big line of dominoes. I just had to hope and believe that they would topple over in the right order.

Fortunately, there were so many things to worry about on this journey that I didn't know quite where to start worrying. This is probably what saved me from going doolally. The only way I could deal with the logistics was to think of the trip in stages and as a series of legs. I could then focus on the detail of each leg without going into meltdown on the number of ifs and buts still remaining in the overall plan.

For several days I sent emails to possible agents based along the 18,000-kilometre route of my journey, with questions about their ability to get me the tickets and reservations I needed. Some of the responses made good sense and others just made me worry more. I chose my team based on little more than how they communicated and the occasional recommendation from other serial rail travellers.

One decision that I didn't have to worry about was who to use for the arrangements in Russia. On my last trip I had found a company called Real Russia, and they remained at the core of organising the front end of the itinerary. After all, if I had no reservation on the Trans-Mongolian or a visa for the Russian Federation, I was going nowhere. Igor would be in charge of my ticketing from Amsterdam as far as Beijing. Anastacia would deal with the red tape, and had a healthy obsession with the details supplied on each of my visa applications. Better that it would be she who found a problem, rather than an official at an embassy.

The other agents would be new to me. Sophie in Beijing was going to try to circumvent the newly introduced Chinese laws on buying train tickets, as a physical visa and passport was now needed for foreigners. Emily in Hanoi was going to get my reservations on the overbooked Vietnamese sleeper trains. In Saigon, Miss Pham Thi Tuong, who insisted that I just call her Vi, would organise bus tickets through to Cambodia, where it turns out the bamboo trains would not be of much use. Mr Soley in

Phenom Pehn had offered to arrange a car from Siam Reap to the Thai border. And back in London, a chap called Dave had access to the Thai and Malaysian railway ticketing systems. He worked at International Rail, which whenever I said it in my mind I thought of as International Rescue – cue the *Thunderbirds* theme music. As a solitary traveller I felt good to have a team like this behind the logistics. I don't think it would have been possible for me to organise this trip 15 years ago without a small army of intermediary travel agents and a lot of fax paper. Possibly even a telex machine.

I have always found it to be a slightly sad aspect of travel that you get to meet brilliant people on the ground who help you sort all your problems and then you never get to see them again. I was really keen to get hold of Alexey, the fixer and guide in Moscow from my last adventure. When I asked Igor about finding him again I must have sounded like an American asking a Londoner if they knew of someone called Tony. I had forgotten it is such a common name, and I could not remember any of his other details. Then by chance I found his card with a local telephone number in the pocket of my Arctic jacket, along with the card of my favourite Uzbek restaurant and a metro ticket. Igor traced him, and I was really pleased to have his services again. Last time we had inspected nuclear bombers together, eaten Armenian dumplings and appreciated the battle paintings of Vasily Vereshchagin. But best of all he had been my key to decoding how Russians think.

I didn't worry too much about my gear until quite close to blast-off. I knew that I had most of it from my last journey, but there were a few aspects that I wanted to fine-tune. By far the biggest and most important of these was my main bag. Having been almost crippled carrying a heavy duffel bag to Shanghai, I needed a better solution. In Edinburgh this meant only one thing, a trip to the temple of luggage that was Jenners department store. Tucked away in a corner of the fourth floor was the entrance to the largest luggage store in the city, and inside was the high priest, a man in his early 40s who was supervising bag-based worship.

I had past form here, and wondered if he would recognise me, but if he did he disguised it well. All around the room were well ordered piles of gleaming bags of every shape and size. My feeling was that if I were to survive a journey of this length without a significant private medical bill, I would need a bag with wheels. It might not sound too cool to be an adventurer using a bag with wheels, but after my last experience this was how it was going to have to be, unless I was going to bring a Sherpa along with me.

I gave a bag I liked the look of a little push, and it floated across the room. This was baggage magic. After wheeling a few bags around the floor in the style of a dog show, the priest became more interested in me and asked me what I was looking for. 'It needs to hold 100 litres, be lockable, snow proof, stable on ice and ideally be strong enough to use as an impromptu chair or table,' I told him.

Without even a hint of surprise at my request he pulled out a few more bags that he felt might meet my needs. These each underwent a road test and a winner finally emerged. I chose a hard-sided silver bag which claimed to have been a bi product of the American space programme's research into kevlar. It was called a 'spinner' on account of having four wheels and being able to travel in every direction with just a flick of its sturdy fold-out handle. The luggage priest took me over to the altar where I presented my credit card to the holy EPOS machine. He was clearly pleased to see someone so appreciative of the products of his religion, and wished me well before attending to a new worshipper.

There were a few more specialist bits of kit on my list. The first of these could only be procured from Russia, but nonetheless I decided to buy it online before I set off. On my last trip I had purchased a tourist version of the famous Russian ushanka hat. But I hankered after the authenticity of a real one. It's the go-to winter hat for all branches of the military. I found a specialist supplier in Volgograd and made the purchase. When I unpacked the parcel, I noticed immediately that I had been promoted since my last adventure. My previous hat had been for a humble soldier in the Red Army, but my new one had the badge of a Soviet Navy admiral. There is actually a practical reason for this. There have always been a number of different grades of material used in the construction of the ushanka. The soldiers had hats made of pressed felt, whereas their commanders had better quality fur, and sometimes leather. Today most of the tourist hats are made using synthetic fur and whilst they are actually very comfy, they are not as warm and durable as the real thing. My new ushanka was made famous to capitalist film goers across the world in 1990 by Sir Sean Connery as Captain Marko Ramius in *The Hunt for Red October*. I only wish that his accent had been more convincing.

My favourite new gadget for this journey was called a Handpresso. It looked like a bicycle pump but was actually a portable espresso coffee machine with a pressure gauge and a coffee pod attached at one end. I practised hard with this at home, as my early technique had frequently resulted in my spraying hot coffee all over the kitchen rather than into my lucky metal explorer's mug.

A few weeks before I was due to set off I visited my long-suffering doctor. Despite trying to look after myself and even improve my fitness for the rigours of adventure, I hadn't been in the best of health for a couple of months and my immune system was a bit hammered. He suggested that I might consider delaying my departure, but once he realised that I was going whatever he said, he started tapping various prescriptions into the old-school computer on his heavily cluttered desk. Whilst he was doing his two-finger typing he asked me to describe my route and listened intently as if a further appraisal of my mental condition might also be needed. I talked him through the journey point to point, and when I got as far as Cambodia he stopped typing and looked up and started asking questions.

It turned out that he had worked as a medical volunteer close to my crossing point on the Thai/Cambodian border, home of the infamous town of Poipet. This place held the top spot on my list of places to worry about for several reasons. The issues here included the presence of drug-resistant malaria and its proximity to an actively disputed border region – or, put simply, a war. It was also judged by most journalists and travellers as the biggest rip-off joint in Southeast Asia, largely run by an unregulated mafia. I thought of it in *Star Wars* terms. Hopefully you have seen the film. This was the Tatooine space port of Mos Eisley. As Obi-Wan tells Luke: 'You will never find a more wretched hive of scum and villainy. We must be cautious.'

Walking out of the pharmacy with a large carrier bag of drugs, I realised that I have two new problems. Firstly, how to carry that many pills, and secondly, how not to get mistaken for a drug dealer when my bags were searched. I carefully copied my prescriptions and medical documents and packed them with the pills in a big plastic box. Surely no self-respecting drug dealer would do this?

Before I depart on any adventure I nearly always have some pretty strange dreams. As I counted down to D-Day on my calendar, they got weirder by the day. What did they mean? I consulted several books on dream analysis, but these weren't just the usual missing your train or being frozen and unable to move on the platform type nightmares. These were dreams involving things from the wildest parts of my imagination coupled with everything that could go wrong on a train. Why was there a giraffe poking his head through the window into the train, and what was the significance of having a phone made out of gold that could not make outgoing calls? Why did I share a bathroom with Bruce Lee? In the spirit of 'better out than in' I figured that it was better to let my subconscious process these hang-ups in the comfort of my own bed rather than in the heart of Siberia.

My first attempt to pack everything into my bags didn't go too well. This was no real surprise to me as I knew that I had too much stuff. People who know about these things tell you to just halve what you have packed, but this didn't work for me. Which half should I throw away? I needed to carry clothes to survive the Siberian winter as well as clothes to deal with the jungles of Southeast Asia. The temperature would vary by as much as 70°C. I contemplated the idea of sending the winter gear home by post, but this was impracticable unless I was going to buy replacement tropical gear in the markets of Vietnam – and I didn't very much fancy the North Vietnamese Army Irregular look.

It turns out there was an exact way to pack my new bag in a way that almost everything fitted in apart from my Flying Scotsman thermos flask and my new hat. It was rather like a special puzzle, and everything had to go in a certain order, a certain way. I decided that I would just have to wear everything that didn't fit in. This might have repercussions in the jungle. I also decided to buy most of my provisions in Moscow, where I would have a helping hand getting extra bags onto the Trans-Mongolian train.

As the departure date loomed there was little else to do. I re-checked all my documents and made copies of my passport and visas. I kept these on a memory stick in case of the worst-case scenario, but I worried about its compatibility with Cambodian Microsoft. In the end I sealed some photocopies in an envelope and hid them in the lining of one of my bags. I'm not a smuggler, but I thought it was a good concealment.

The restless mood that I suspect most people feel before they set off on their big trip can be counter-productive. I certainly suffer from this. I dwelled on the thoughts of failure, of not achieving what I have set out to do. I think it's human nature. I just needed to get going. Final checks: ushanka, yes; bags, yes; passport, yes; sense of humour, yes. I locked the door, opened it, checked for the third time that I had turned the gas off, locked the door once more and headed to Edinburgh Waverley Station to catch a train to Newcastle and the ferry to Ijmuiden.

'I think we might be going a bridge too far.'

Lt-General Sir Frederick Arthur Montague 'Boy' Browning

Three: Market Garden

Day Two, Amsterdam, Holland
Distance travelled so far: 693 km

Amsterdam time (GMT +1)

Station	Arrival	Departure
Amsterdam		19:04
Koln	23:10	23:13
Dusseldorf	23:35	23:37

I have a day to kill in a dull and damp Amsterdam before catching the night train to Warsaw. Gathering my belongings from the bowels of the bus that has delivered me to the city from the port of Ijmuiden, I zip my down jacket up and make for the station as directly as I dare without being run over by a tram. Outside the station stands a single enormous Christmas tree surrounded by a mixture of tourists, possible drug dealers and assorted undesirables.

To me Amsterdam is a Marmite kind of place. You either love its relaxed way of living or see nothing but the slightly depressing underbelly of life here. When I was a student I'd had a few big nights out in the city that seemed like fun at the time. Back then waking up with no money and thick head was slightly amusing, but I'm less easily seduced today. In the summer it's a wonderful place to sip a beer outside, overlooking a canal and the carnage of foreign tourists meeting Dutch cyclists for the first time. But on a cold and grey winter's day, I just huddle in coffee shops biding my time. Outside, the big businesses of drugs, prostitution, stag parties and clog sales carry on regardless of the bleakness and light rain.

The first few hours of any new adventure always seem to trouble me. It's the transition from normality to the excitement and acceptance of the unknown. It's relearning how to flick that switch in my head so that I can just exist in the present. Fortunately, the present day in Amsterdam is full of weird and interesting people, and it quickly consumes me.

Today I decide to embrace being a tourist, and I buy a ticket for a canal cruise. A warm boat is definitely preferable to the damp streets. Once inside I find a table and sit down with a map and the headphones that have been provided. Moments before we cast off a bunch of well-tanned men crowd down the gangplank. I'm joined by a Brazilian football player who introduces himself as Matheus, complete with his small but devoted entourage of supporters. I tell him that's my name too, and he is suddenly my brother. I'm not big in terms of football knowledge, and I don't speak a word of Portuguese, but I follow the instructions given and hold one end of a big flag that we wave at people on the streets above us.

I wonder if Matheus is really famous, but don't have time to ask him what he thinks of the Gulfstream 550. He is here to play against Germany next week, so before we part I wish him good luck. I was going to make a joke based on *The Great Escape*, but I think better of it.

The fast food culture in Amsterdam intrigues me, especially the open-fronted shops selling ready-heated meals from little metal hatches in the wall. I can't work out what's behind each door. I let fate decide today if I end up with a cheese croquette or a weird-tasting sausage. But instead I end up with a slice of molten pizza that's hotter than the sun. The law here seems to be that adding mayonnaise to fast food is compulsory. This has of course now been made famous by the classic 1994 Quentin Tarantino movie *Pulp Fiction*. I slather my pizza in the white gunge from the big dispenser and devour it as best I can without getting burned by the napalm-like cheese.

From the outside, Amsterdam Centraal is a grand station, built in an impressive Gothic Renaissance style. It's the Disney castle-like building that dominates this part of the city. Inside, however, after years of development work it still looks a bit dodgy to me. Statistics say that it's safer than many other European railway stations, but the look and the edgy feel of the place put me very much on my guard. I have never seen anything go wrong, but always feel I'm riding out my good fortune here. Today I don't linger as I pick up some groceries and recover my bags from the left luggage place. A helpful lady in the

InterCity office confirms all is good with the EN447, my train this evening. With nothing else to do I decide that it's safer, if colder, to wait up on the platform.

The utilitarian plastic shelter on platform 7 allows me to hide from the wind coming off the North Sea passing through the open ends of the station. My metal bench is cold, and sitting soon becomes uncomfortable. With some time to kill I wander down to the noticeboard, where I find some clever little drawings showing where each carriage is on each train for the day. I understand the technical term is a 'train composition' board. The irony of course, is that anyone trying to find their coach in hurry would never spot it. Fortune favours the passenger who is not in a rush.

When the Euro Night 447 or *Jan Kiepura* finally pulls into the station I'm quickly on board the right carriage without any fuss. From the dark and cosy interior of my compartment I can watch the other passengers trying to find their home for the night. It's a long train with a mixture of rolling stock, mainly gleaming red German DB and older-looking blue and white Polish PKP carriages. The train will be split up several times along its route tonight, serving cities right across north-west Europe. My carriage has seen better days, but inside I have all the mod cons I need for a good night: a comfy single berth, a sink, power sockets, air conditioning, and a hidden cupboard behind a mirror stocked with railway survival rations consisting mainly of water and chocolate biscuits.

The train sets off so slowly that at first movement is imperceptible without a reference point outside. You could certainly walk faster along the platform with a pet tortoise. But gathering momentum with each metre we move forwards, gradually overcoming the inertia of the train's massive weight. Eventually we break free of the confines of the station and I find myself in 'railway darkness' as we rumble across a raised section of track above the city. On a sleeper train it can be pretty embarrassing to arrive in a station when you are in a state of undress or sleep, so I turn off all the lights off in my compartment to remain hidden from anyone on the platform. There is a blind that pulls down from the top of the window, but if you close it you lose your connection with the outside world. Once the train is out of the station I just let my eyes gradually adjust to the darkness outside; the flashing of railway signal lights and illumination of provincial towns and roads by dim streetlights.

Sitting comfortably on the neatly folded blankets of my berth, I check my watch and study a printed copy of the train timetable. Exactly one hour and six minutes after leaving Amsterdam the train is scheduled to reach the river at Arnhem. I want to be part of that moment, almost as though it is the start line for my challenge of crossing so many rail bridges and nearly 18,000 kilometres in the weeks ahead.

The railway bridge at Arnhem today actually crosses over the nearby River Ijssel, near to where the modern John Frost Bridge stands on the Rhine. As we approached I couldn't spot any hidden Panzer tanks, but I could definitely imagine them being there. Right on time, first the modern station in the centre of Arnhem, then a bridge of huge curved spans and girders. The distinctive bridge-rumbling noise of metal on metal underneath us in the darkness. The swishing sound outside the carriage as we sweep past each metal column in the span.

At a pre-departure curry with Mark Hudson, my Arnhem expert friend, I had been tested on my knowledge of the battle. The question came up on the best way to capture a bridge, to which I didn't know the answer. This is a vital piece of trivia in the sweet spot between military history and bridges in any pub quiz. In case, like me, you need to know how, the answer is that you take both ends at exactly the same time.

I remember how excited I had been to watch *A Bridge Too Far* for the very first time. This would have been a couple of years after its release, maybe in 1979. The film has a 15 certificate in the UK today, but I think back then it might have been classified as an AA. The giant and slightly scary colonel who ran the school cadet force screened it on his state-of-the-art 16mm projector one Saturday night to a room full of underage and highly impressionable junior school boys.

We were so excited we just didn't know what to do. From my wonky wooden chair in the assembly room, I stared agog at the cinema screen. I was mesmerised by the coolness and camaraderie between Edward Fox and Michael Caine as they drove towards the front of the armoured column to lead XXX Corps in the general's Willys jeep. They prepared to face the enemy in the style of two good friends bumping into colleagues on a trip to the local golf club. To this day I still very much enjoy this scene, but my favourite moment now is actually when Field Marshal Model decides that the Allies have landed just to capture him at his country house HQ. Forgoing the remainder of his fine lunch, he tells his aide to get his car ready – and adding to his orders, after further thought, not to forget his cigars. Very classy.

Once over the bridge my train passes seamlessly into Germany, where it weaves along the industrial valley of the Rhine. With no other sightseeing planned for the evening, I unpack and dig out my secret key, to help myself to an extra pillow from a locked berth. Then I decide to open the window with it too. I have a bit of a track record with train windows, and this was in hindsight another huge window-based mistake. Once I have it open I can't shut it again whatever I try; the heavy seal prevents it from closing. I don't mind the cold so much or even a touch of snow coming in, but the wind now loudly whistles through the gap and in my little compartment it is unsurprisingly as loud as an express train. If you have not heard about this key before, many railway carriages outside the United Kingdom use a guard's key based on a shape that is coincidentally exactly the same as a humble British Gas meter cupboard key.

Before turning in I carefully set the locks on my door, and pull down the window blind before lying down on my narrow but pretty comfy berth. I realise that I need my earplugs, and quickly locate them in a little bag I have for things I might need in the night. Sleep doesn't come very easily, so for quite some time I count imaginary parachutists with camouflaged helmets and Sten guns falling from the sky. I must stop eating Dutch pizzas. God only knows what they put in them.

Day Three, Poznan, Poland
Distance travelled so far: 1,692 km

Warsaw time (GMT +1)

Station	Arrival	Departure
Dortmund	00:29	00:32
Berlin	06:47	06:50
Poznin	09:24	09:38
Konin	10:26	10:27
Kutno	11:07	11:08
Warsaw Centralna	12:17	

The next morning there is a gentle knock on the door at about 8.00am. The friendly Polish conductor called Michael appears with a little plastic tray bearing a meal that he believes to be called breakfast: a sodden cheese sandwich, a long-life croissant, a small block of plastic-wrapped processed cheese, some crackers and a carton of colorants and E numbers that make up an orange-coloured drink. It is the sort of food you would eat to survive on, but otherwise avoid at all costs. Returning my ticket to me, he makes no small talk about how I had slept, or if I had seen the bridge at Arnhem before turning in last night. His main duty is to explain in railway English that the train is now running 40 minutes early. Forty minutes early? How does that work? Have people missed their train this morning because the driver is in a hurry to reach his wife and family in Warsaw? I know PKP compensate people who are delayed, but I wondered if it did the same for those missing a connection owing to their train departing early.

Michael returns once more with a cup of acrid instant coffee in a polystyrene cup. As soon as he has left me, I waste no time pouring it down my little sink, and head out to find the restaurant carriage which hopefully has been added at the Polish border. I don't have to walk far: through the pneumatic doors and there it is. A carriage where real espresso coffee is served in thick china cups, and eggs can be freshly scrambled. This one seems quite typical of a European restaurant carriage. At one end is the kitchen and a place you can stand to order and pay for food, then down one side are small tables and high chairs, with low seats on the other side. The waiter takes down your order on the back of a beer mat and they bring the food out to your table when it is ready. Other than the sway of the carriage you might forget that you are actually dining on a train. Breakfast is one of my favourite experiences on the rails. It's that combination of comfort food, news from fellow travellers and new scenery, as you have travelled over maybe 500 km since the view when the sun last set.

Last night I must have only had a couple of hours of the decent sleep. I need to make the adjustment to living on a train. In a few days' time I will have learned to screen out platform announcements and hopefully even to find some of the alien train noises a little soporific; much like people who live near airports but can no longer hear the planes.

Outside the train this morning there is a new and subtly different world. Not much snow yet, but it is seriously frosty and cold. Trans-European rail travel is fast and efficient these days. Blink and you miss the once formal frontiers that signal the differences of people, places, landscape and nationality. What I could see out the window this morning was the prosperity of modern-day Poland. Fields, yes – but also family cars, supermarkets, modern houses and freshly built roads. The soundtrack to my morning is 'Love Over Gold' by Dire Straits.

With the excitement of breakfast out the way, I get myself packed up in case we arrive even more than 40 minutes early. I'm not too worried, though, as the worst that can happen today will be that I will miss my stop and end up in Warsaw Zachodnia, the station on the eastern side of the city that the train will terminate in. The guard seems well drilled in how to get the right passengers off at each of the stops passing through Warsaw, and as soon as we have passed Warsaw Wschodnia he positions me in a line by the door.

Warsaw Centralna is a single enormous booking hall building built on top of a subterranean bunker. Its design is very Eastern Bloc, and it is getting to the age where it probably needs demolishing to make way for a modern station. Every day thousands of passengers dart through its labyrinth of underground shop-lined passageways and tunnels to find their trains. On the plus side it is warm, but on the minus side it is hard to navigate and has a distinctive smell of urine and stale bagels.

My immediate challenge is to get all my bags as well as myself on the escalator to take me from the platform and up into the maze of tunnels. It isn't just my own life that I am taking into my hands by doing this; one slip and my enormous bag will tombstone its way back down to the platform, taking everyone in its path with it. But once on the level it's in its element and I marvel at how manoeuvrable it is. Ditching my cargo bag was a great decision.

My hotel would have been easy to find were I on the surface. I pop up briefly like a POW tunnel digger in need of a reference point above. A compass might have been helpful. I can see the 1980s-built tower of the Marriot from the booking hall, but between me and it is an enormous snowy highway with no obvious crossing points. Back down in the caverns I am quickly disoriented again, and I seek help from a lady who runs a bakery and speaks a bit of English. She gives me a complex set of directions and I set off with renewed vigour to find her route out. I am quite surprised finally to haul myself up some stairs and emerge right outside where I need to be.

I have decided to stay at the Marriot for two reasons. Firstly, with the right tunnel route mastered it is a short walk to the station; and secondly it was featured in a cult 1980s BBC television series called *A Very Peculiar Practice*. At the time, it was the newest and best business hotel in Warsaw. I think hotels should market themselves better by using interest in the films that they have appeared in. The one-off episode entitled *A Very Polish Practice* featured Peter Davidson and David Troughton, both at the top of their game.

I need sleep but decide to just keep going, so I find an interesting-looking restaurant to try a lunch of traditional Polish food. This mostly involves dumplings and pickled cabbage, but the dark beer tastes pretty good.

Fortified by my meal, my next stop is the Polish National Army Museum. Outside sits a serious quantity of Cold War junk. Ballistic missile launchers, now without strategic purpose, are lined up in the snow and just rusting away. I think I even found the version that they used in the classic 1985 comedy film *Spies Like Us*.

Walking back towards my hotel along the wide frozen main street, I can't quite make my mind up about Warsaw. Although it's such a bleak place, the locals seem very friendly. They seem to compensate for the oppressive climate and the acres of Brutalist concrete.

Reaching Warsaw feels like an important milestone in my journey, even though I have still covered less than 2,000 km. It's a final staging post, a place where everything from this place onward will be alien, weird and interesting. The language here sounds very different, and the food certainly is. But it's more than my environment: it's me. Just a couple of nights on the rails and I already feel relaxed in my new way of life; living in the moment and with no time to think about anything else. Rail adventure is a drug, and I am high on it.

Four: The Praga Firefighters' Co-Operative

Day Three, Warsaw, Poland
Distance travelled so far: 1,995 km

The lobby of the Marriot hotel is an impressive place, and I don't really belong in it. I stand out as the only man not wearing a suit, and none of the men in suits are wearing boots like mine, with a Siberian capability. What had I been thinking to sign myself up to an alternative slice of Warsaw nightlife, when I could just be relaxing and drinking rather good local beer?

I don't know what my contact looks like, and he doesn't know me, but when he arrives it takes about five seconds to work out that I'm his student for the evening. His name is Wojtek. He is a serious man in his late twenties, dressed in a big parka jacket, the arm pockets stuffed with pens and pencils. He introduces himself in quite a formal way, and explains that his other students have cancelled today. I am the only trainee tonight and we will be going out on patrol together, alone. That's right – 'patrol'!

47

The hotel concierge must have left his post to have kittens, for outside the big revolving entrance door isn't a car, but a Soviet fire engine parked where his limousines should be. You could only smile when you saw that fire engine for the first time. It was from both a different time and a distant political regime. Known as a Zuk, it is a Polish design based on a Russian GAZ-M20 Pobeda. Looking at it its small and simple boxlike construction, you would guess it had been built on the instruction of Stalin in the 1950s. There is probably some truth in this, but they were in fact produced well into the 1980s and are still popular with farmers across Poland today.

Wojtek unlocks the doors and as I clamber up into the surprisingly springy co-pilot's seat I can see that he is studying me carefully from behind his round metal spectacles. He seems to me to be a quiet and reserved chap – not the sort of person that you would seek if you were recruiting a team of firemen. He also has that Eastern Bloc affliction of not finding it easy to smile easily in public.

Settling me into my new role as second in command of a Polish fire engine, he shows me where all the main switches and buttons are. There are four, or five if you include the ignition switch. There is a good view out of the flat windscreen, obscured only by a kitsch East German clock on the dashboard and a football scarf of Legia Warszawa dangling from the rear-view mirror. Behind me where our crew of four fit and eager firemen should have been sitting, are a range of helmets and miscellaneous pieces of ancient-looking firefighting equipment. I only hope that we won't be needing to use them tonight.

Wojtek's briefing is succinct and to the point: 'We will go now. First, we will test the performance of the fire engine, then we will go to Praga to see the ghetto.' How could anyone refuse such an offer? After a couple of attempts, the engine of the mighty Zuk splutters into life and, the heavy handbrake released, we gyrate slowly out of the car park in the direction of the Vistula river. Our Zuk is equipped with a 2120cc petrol engine, but only three forward gears. Worse still the independent front suspension makes it feel like a pram, and every time Wojtek changes gear the Zuk tips forwards in an alarming manner, causing me to lean back as if I could balance out the changing forward momentum. Braking is an even more alarming procedure and I have no idea how close we are to the limits of adhesion. As we accelerate down the highway and across the Swietokrzyski Bridge I desperately try to locate a seatbelt, or even a piece of rope, but there is nothing to attach myself to the seat with. I have to accept that my fate is in Wojtek's hands. On the plus side, if we crash it will be over pretty quickly. But there is no time to dwell on such negative thoughts, as he jabs the brakes hard and we snake to a halt at some traffic lights before making an illegal U-turn to get back on our route to the edgy district of Praga, known to some as Warsaw's version of the Bermuda Triangle.

I had found the fire fighter experience on the internet. The deal was that I would be shown some historic off the beaten path places and some good drinking joints. The sort of places that tourists would never find. I was reminded of Alex Garland's epic book *The Beach* and Richard's line 'I just feel like everyone tries to do something different, but you always wind up doing the same damn thing.'

It gets dark; Praga definitely looks like the sort of neighbourhood that you need to know your onions in. I notice that Wojtek always parks carefully and the right way around – I assume just in case a quick getaway might be needed. Praga was not bombed flat like much of Warsaw during the Second World War, and its buildings still retain a ghetto construction of communal passageways leading into huge courtyards. There are bullet holes in concrete walls, cobblestones and wooden gates. Life here has changed, but literally only in the last few years. Praga is now seen as a hip and trendy address, a Polish Harlem, or maybe the Bronx.

After an evening looking at various places of underground and historic interest, including a few calls into bars to investigate non-existent fires, we head back to the fire station. This is a bar called OSP Saska Kspa. I thought that calling it a fire station was possibly a joke, but as we lean into a tight turn down a narrow side street, in front of us is a low industrial building and outside it are three other fire engines. We park up next to them and pack up the Zuk just in case an emergency callout comes in whilst we are having a drink.

Inside there are a few normal-looking men and women in a social context, but rather strangely wearing items of firefighting uniform in combination with smart clothes. An obligatory photograph is required, and for this I am handed a red plastic helmet and a pair of goggles. As not much English is spoken, I wondered if I am actually being induced into a new cult movement. I decide that they all look nice enough, though, and happily wear my new items of firefighting uniform. I decide that I will remain a cult member until they ask me to do something weird. They all seem happy enough in their firefighting world, and their spiritual leader is clearly delighted to see me joining in. He looks on approvingly whilst I am induced into the new religion.

All good things come to an end and at closing time Wotjek drives me back to my hotel, once again driving right up to the front door to be sure I make it home safely. I wish him well, returning my goggles before climbing down to meet a small group of onlookers. 'Fire patrol,' I tell them as I head for the warmth of the lobby, like it's an everyday part of Warsaw civic duty.

Resisting the urge to head for the bar, I head straight to my room and decide to start repacking bags for the next leg of the trip. Experience has taught me how hard it is to open a suitcase in the compartment of a moving train, so you need all the important stuff in a smaller bag, where you can get to it. Satisfied with my efforts I turn off the lights and flop onto the

51

enormous and decadent Western bed, realising that this might be the last big bed I will sleep in for quite some time. Not being able to switch off, I start to think about what lies ahead on the next leg – Russians, visas, red tape and even wheel changes. But there is a nagging doubt in the back of my mind. A reality check is needed. I have a Mr Benn moment.

Mr Benn was a popular children's television programme broadcast in the United Kingdom in the early 1970s. It came from an age when kids' programmes were a series of animated drawings with a reassuring adult voiceover. In every episode Mr Benn visits a fancy-dress shop where a bespectacled man wearing a fez magically appears, to suggest Mr Benn might like to try a new costume on. Then from the door of the changing room he is transported to a faraway place. He might be a pirate, a caveman, a wizard, or even a spaceman. But back through the door once more he is in the shop again, where he changes into his trademark suit and bowler hat. Mr Benn was a long way ahead of his time. He was a diplomat, an environmentalist and an all-round nice chap. You were always sad that his latest adventure was over and he was back in the real world. Walking back to his home at number 52 Festive Road, he always found a small memento to remind him that his adventure had really happened.

Have I imagined my firefighting adventure? Did that really just happen? I fumble around in the darkness of the room looking for my phone. On the camera roll is a picture of me wearing a helmet, with the Zuk outside the fire station. It has really happened and this isn't a vodka-infused fantasy – now I know how Mr Benn felt; but all the same I really should get back on the rails.

Five: Polonez

Day Four, Warsaw, Poland
Distance travelled so far: 1,995 km

Warsaw time (GMT +1)

Station	Arrival	Departure
Warsaw Centralna		15:45
Minsk Mazowiecki	16:26	16:27
Siedlce	17:00	17:01
Lukow	17:18	17:19
Terespol	18:24	19:32
Brest	22:18	00:13

The D10 *Polonez* presents the anorak rail adventurer with a small problem of detail; a seemingly random outcome as to who will operate the train on the day you travel. Some days it is run by Polish Railways and on other days it is a Russian Railways train. It should rotate every day, but that's hard to calculate accurately when you book far ahead, and it's hidden from the timetable. It's not one to lose any sleep over, but there are a few differences in the carriages depending on your love of opening windows versus air conditioning and old versus new. But as this is outside of my control, I decide to embrace the positives of whichever train is running today.

The underground platform at Warsaw Centralna is warm, and could even be described as snug compared to the outside world. I feel very much in control of things down here, mainly because the signs and train information are excellent, and also as the platform conductors speak a little English. At the bottom of the escalator there is a helpful composition board. With this information I'm able to stand at exactly the right place on the platform and wait for my carriage to come to me, rather than me dash after it, which is usually what happens. The *Polonez* is made up mainly of regular carriages which are just going as far as Terespol at the hard border with Belarus. This is the end of the line for all the passengers without the right paperwork and passports. But the train also has some sleeper carriages that will eventually cross into Belarus and onward into the Russian Federation.

The train approaches the platform at dead slow speed, almost as if the driver doesn't want to arrive a second early. In the tunnel of the station, the noise of the powerful engine is all-encompassing, a dull rumble of train thunder that drowns out every other noise. I'm a bit confused, as the carriage number in front of me isn't the one I'm looking for.

Panic over. This isn't my train, but the one before, bound for the airport. A couple of friendly staff wander up and down, reassuring passengers that they are in the right place for the D10. The next train that pulls up has a lot of quite rough-looking green seated carriages, but up front there are two or three sleepers that look marginally better. It's a Polish train today, and that suits me. Polish carriages often have windows that you can open whereas the Russians like it toasty hot inside, so I might getter a better night's sleep on this one.

Once on board, the first hurdle is to find my compartment. I can see no obvious cabin numbers as I push my bags awkwardly in front of me down the corridor. In a moment of junior rail explorer panic I declare sheepishly that I'm lost and seek pity from one of the other passengers with less luggage behind me. He shrugs his shoulders and points forwards. Then I get lucky and see a number that corresponds to my reservation coupon. It's right at the forward end of the carriage at the other end from where I have boarded. On the plus side, it's a short walk to the toilet, but on the minus side I'm next to where people often hang around smoking. I bundle my bags in first and follow behind.

I like what they have done inside – a decent-sized single bed, a sink under a little shelf, and a power socket hidden behind a mirrored cupboard together with some PKP rations. An indication of first class, or sole occupancy here, is that you get an upgraded menu including a Prince wafer biscuit and a Scooby Doo orange drink. Unlike in a Chinese carriage you don't need to be a trained plumber to adjust the central heating either: turning a simple knob covers the convection holes above the pipework and cools things down. I think that it is actually a really old carriage, but it has been refurbished with carpet and painted surfaces to keep in touch with the last decade.

It's a bit gloomy inside, but we are still sitting at an underground platform. Whilst I'm familiarising myself with my new environment the conductor pops her head in and introduces herself. Her name is Lena and she speaks reasonably good English. Once she is happy I'm the right passenger in the right place she asks me for my ticket, which she puts into a special place for my compartment in her folder. With the business done, she leaves me to it.

After a few announcements in what I assume to be Polish, we pull out of Centrana. There is a seemingly good atmosphere on the train and the compartment doors are mainly open. The Russian couple next door play traditional music on some sort of ancient cassette machine, and Lena has put the kettle on in her cramped quarters at the far end of the carriage.

I once heard the world-wise traveller Alan Whicker explain to an audience that anyone could be uncomfortable; you just had to choose not to be. Having always taken this advice to heart, I had a bag of kit to make sure my journey was immediately more enjoyable, and first out of it this afternoon was my trusty Trans-Siberian insulated metal mug. Anyone could be uncomfortable with a plastic one that occasionally melts and tastes a bit nasty. But instead my shiny metal one made hot drinks a total pleasure. It's jasmine tea today and it's making me feel like I'm much further east than I actually am. I'm carrying a plastic box with a variety of tea bags, so the ceremony of making decent cup is as simple as a trip to the samovar with my lucky metal mug. The only thing I need to get used to is life without is milk, so I have moved onto mainly herbal and flavoured varieties.

Once settled in, I complete a quick review of my paperwork and fish out a printed copy of the timetable. I notice that on this route there are in fact two places called Minsk. We have just left the Polish one, a small town with a massive supermarket, and we don't arrive at the capital of Belarus until 3.07 tomorrow morning. It looks like we will arrive at the border between 19:22 and 23:33, but I think one of those times is GMT +1 and the other GMT +3. I very much doubt that there is even a remote chance of sleep until we have had our grilling from the border security and the wheels have been swapped for the wider Russian tracks. The evening ahead promises a combination of unexciting paperwork and much hanging about in the engine sheds of Brest.

Without warning the main carriage lights are turned on and the relaxed and intimate feel of the place immediately vanishes. It's all business now, and Lena pokes her head into each compartment to announce our imminent arrival at the border: 'Terespol, Terespol.' The atmosphere changes to one of silent apprehension of what might be in store for us.

Our first stop is the Polish border station, where most people from the other carriages leave the train. A policeman comes aboard and checks each compartment to see that we each have a valid passport and visa for Belarus. More forms are handed out and I complete them in my best handwriting, hoping to be given extra credit and possibly a sticky-backed gold star for good homework.

Outside on the platform it is deserted now. All I can see are CCTV cameras and razor wire. The engine idles as we sit here for more than half an hour before finally getting under way. We edge slowly over the long bridge that crosses the River Bug. All I can make out are the occasional burning cigarette ends from soldiers guarding either side. This is definitely a significant bridge of the Cold War. If I-Spy published a book of important Eastern Bloc railway bridges, then this would certainly be in it. The views are apparently very nice here in the daytime, but in darkness I'm just drawn to close-up glimpses of the bridge and its heavy defences.

Waiting, ready to greet us, at the platform of the Belarus side of the frontier is the next batch of officials. Dressed in dull grey disruptive camouflage uniforms, they march up to each carriage in ready-sized detachments and climb on board, slamming all doors for dramatic effect. The handguns here are no longer made of Austrian polymer, and the rifles that the soldiers carry now descend from Mikhail Kalashnikov's original design. Our passport photographs are studied and there is much staring and comparison before they are taken away for further inspection. We wait again, nothing to see or hear apart from the occasional slamming of doors and the marching of boots up and down the icy platform. Then without warning, a short trundle into the station at Brest without passports, but with all the security people still on board the train. You just have to trust that they know the drill and go with it.

Eventually a lady captain comes to the door of my compartment, smiles and politely hands me back my passport without any questions. Just when I think it's all done, another woman dressed in combats arrives to search my compartment and asks me to step out into the corridor whilst she pokes around. I wonder what she is looking for. She must know all the best places in a railway carriage to conceal something, as she gets her torch and screwdriver out and thoroughly checks every conceivable place, and probably many that I don't know about, but as I'm in the corridor I don't get to discover them. Once her search is complete she asks me if I have any alcohol, so I proudly show her my rather nice bottle of Georgian red wine that I had found in a Warsaw off licence. She didn't seem as excited by my choice as I had been, but decides that I am unlikely to be a serious black market booze smuggler. With that done, I'm pleased to learn that I'm going to be admitted to Belarus.

Once inside Belarus there will be no hard border when we cross into Russia later in the night. My Belarus immigration paperwork admits me to Russia as well, and I will surrender this only when I reach the Mongolian border. It's like an Eastern Bloc version of the Schengen area. I also learned from the visa process in London that once you had a Russian visa issued, a Belarus transit visa was pretty much a certainty. It must take the pressure off the Belarus embassy, knowing that Moscow has already granted you their full red tape blessing.

The final call of duty at the border is to change the wheels, a process that takes a couple of hours. The carriages are indelicately shunted off to a huge shed where each is lifted off its bogies by special hydraulic jacks and new bogies are pulled underneath. Whilst this is going on I try to pretend it's all normal inside my carriage, now swinging high above the ground with nothing underneath. Meanwhile manly men mill about underneath the carriages wielding heavy equipment protected just by orange vests and lit cigarettes.

Once the wider Russian gauge wheels are attached to the each of the carriages they are shunted back onto the main line. Back in the station, a small army of Belarusian babushkas are allowed onto the train to sell their food and drinks to passengers. Business will be brisk, as they know only too well that this train has no restaurant carriage, and it is another 14 hours until we reach Moscow.

I let the first babushka who arrives at my door into my compartment without much thinking about it. I don't know how to select babushkas from appearance as they all look the same and we don't have a common language. We both sit on my bed whilst she shows me the contents of her bag. I'm a little concerned that she has closed the door to my compartment, but I assume that this is to keep any of her competitors out.

For a moment I can almost imagine being sold fine carpets or rare trinkets that once belonged to Tsar Nicholas II, but as soon as the bag is opened my illusion is shattered. There is no smell of incense or fine fragrances from the silk route. More the aroma of fried chicken and greasy newspaper. I like the idea of some cheese blinis, and some salted boiled potatoes together with pickles. Adding a couple of Russian beers to the pile of paper parcels on my bed, I get out my phone and calculate the bill in roubles, which is based on hand signals and the calculator on her mobile phone, and convert it to pounds sterling. I'm about to spend about as much on this takeaway as a good meal in a restaurant at home. Alarm bells ring and I suggest a much lower price. Half the beer and the blinis go back in her bag, and the price goes down by two thirds. Eventually the blinis are back out, and it's about half the original price. We have a deal, and once paid with crisp Polish bank notes my bedmate quickly vanishes into the night.

Once we are moving again I relax a bit and enjoy my late-night platform food feast in the relative solitude of my compartment. I have worked out that the design of the Polish sleeper cabins makes them feel more like little burrows than the Russian carriage cabins, which are slightly more traditional and open plan.

It is fairly quiet on board the train now, as passengers settle down for the evening. Lena does her late-night rounds to check on everyone, which is nice. She gives me a quick lecture on keeping my door locked at night – at least I'm guessing that is what she has said, as we don't have more than a few words of German in common. Or maybe she was telling me to keep the chain on in future to keep stray babushkas out of my compartment?

I'm pretty confused by the timetable, and guessing Belarus may have a time zone of its own that I didn't know about – but it's academic, as the train finishes in Moscow tomorrow so I can't miss my stop, at least, I don't think I can ...

Day Five, Smolensk, Russian Federation

Distance travelled so far: 2,885 km

Moscow time (GMT +3)

Station	Arrival	Departure
Minsk	03:50	04:20
Orsha	06:37	06:54
Smolensk	08:09	08:14
Vyazma	09:54	10:17
Moscow	13:05	

I like to get into a routine on board a train, and getting up as soon as I wake is part of my drill. My first priority is to use the limited facilities before others wake. On board the D10 the toilets are a bit primitive, but clean enough to be bearable for a day or two. Train bathrooms have limited space, and their designers seem to have assumed no one will ever need to have a shave or wash anything more than just their hands. My solution is to carry a bag that hooks onto the door and opens up like a cabinet so I can find all the things inside. The only other thing needed is water to brush my teeth, and I have a little bottle for this, which forms part of my kit along with a fast-drying towel, which many would describe as a flannel. With my ablutions complete, I can head back to my compartment and make it up for daytime use.

With my bedding packed up and a bit of reorganisation of the limited space, my next priority is to get some coffee on the go. There is no samovar in this carriage, but Lena has a kettle and is happy to provide hot water to order. This morning I use my Handpresso on a train for the first time. It's a device that Lena is clearly disturbed by and when I bring it to her she has no idea what it is. Perhaps to her it looks like a weapon, and she is partly right as the caffeine is weapons grade. I proudly demonstrate it to her, but I can't convince her that it's a gadget for common good. She looks at me like I might be an evil sorcerer as I fill the reservoir with hot water and leave her to continue reading her Russian gossip magazine.

Fortified by the buzz of a strong and thick steaming coffee in my lucky metal mug, I set about my chores for the morning whilst listening to some unplugged Eric Clapton. Once I have tidied the table I get out the fat paperwork file which contains a plastic pocket for each leg of the trip. I always feel better knowing exactly what is going on in the hours ahead. It's a kind of a one on one briefing to myself of the day's activities. Next, I pull out the map and try to work out where we are. Most of the names make little sense but I can orientate the map using the position of the sun and the time of day, then guess about speed and distance from the last known place. This is very satisfying and makes me feel like a proper explorer. All I need is a pocket watch and a pith helmet and maybe the Explorers Club would admit me.

With my work done I have time to just stare out of the window whilst enjoying more coffee. Today it has become properly wintry. To begin with there is a hanging frost in the air and the world outside is totally frozen. The landscape is rural and remote. But the rising sun gradually melts the ice hanging from branches in the trees, and my window is quickly splattered with falling slush.

Taking a snapshot of how things are going, I conclude that I feel great today. Everything is running to plan, and I am alone and inside the Russian Federation. Unsupported, isolated – and happy that I can get by just fine by myself. There must be something about self-sufficiency in the zen of rail adventure.

When we are about two hours away from Moscow, signs of city life start to emerge. First of all, dirt tracks become roads, an occasional hut becomes a row of houses complete with compounds to keep dogs. The railway has obviously provided the catalyst for development. Things have been built around it. As we get closer to the city the trees are replaced by ramshackle huts next to the tracks. Then the huts become blocks of flats, and the fields are transformed into industrial ground. The buildings gain height, gradually metamorphosing into gleaming Stalinist-styled skyscrapers.

Our railway line joins many others as we circle the western edge of the inner city and there are now dozens of trains all around us. Right on time the pale blue and orange Russian diesel locomotive that has been pulling us blows its horn, and we slowly approach the platforms of Moscow Belorusskaya station. Small crowds have gathered here to welcome their friends and family, and they are dressed like characters in the classic Cold War movie *Ice Station Zebra*. In the well heated interior of the train I have failed to notice the drop in the temperature outside.

Lena helps passengers down onto the iced-up platform, and when it's my turn I put one foot on the platform to test my grip. I slip wildly, but hang on to Lena and the metal handle of the carriage. Gathering my balance, I try to look like I do this all the time. I say goodbye to her and pull my bags past the porters and towards the taxi touts standing in the courtyard outside the main building, wearing leather jackets and fur hats.

At this moment I have a luggage brainwave. What if I were to invent a set of ice skate blades that could be attached to luggage by bungee straps? They would cut through the snow and into the ice underneath. Maybe you could even then lie down on your case like it were a toboggan? I make a mental note to get on to the patent office when I get back home, assuming of course that I will make it back home.

Back in the present, I'm pleased to find that a driver has come to meet me, as some of the tout drivers look like extras from a Russian version of a Mad Max movie. He doesn't help me with my bags but walks away expecting me to keep up with him, out of the station, down a side street across a road and down another turn. Are we walking to the hotel? Just when I'm about to go on strike, we arrive at his quite modern Lada which is absolutely covered in dirty snow and ice. In the back seat I put my seatbelt on and hope this car handles well on the frozen roads.

Moscow traffic can be amazingly bad. The rush hour seems to have already started, but my driver has some cunning shortcuts. The only trouble is getting on and off the expressways, where I'm convinced someone will plough into the back of us. But we make good progress and it takes less than an hour to reach my base, a modern two or three-star business hotel in Sokolniki, a suburb in the north-east of the city.

My timetable gives me a couple of days to relax and prepare for the next leg before getting onto the weekly Trans-Mongolian train to Beijing. This is the big one, the longest single train of my journey, covering over 7,600 km in six days. Often when people talk about travel on the Trans-Siberian railway they are actually using the Trans-Mongolian route, as Beijing is a more useful destination to many than Vladivostok. But the line is the same all the way to

Ulan Ude on day four, so on the 'Trans-Mong' you get to experience some of the 'Trans-Sib' route too. It's good to have a few days living on a train before embarking on such a big leg of the journey. I feel I have built inner confidence from the experience thus far, and once I have caught up on my sleep I will be ready for Siberia.

Six: Bunker 42

Day Six, Moscow, Russian Federation
Distance travelled so far: 3,258 km

It's still dark outside as I eat my buffet breakfast in the brightly lit cavernous dining room of the hotel. The staff are indifferent, trained not to smile and to avoid doing anything unless instructed to do so by someone in command. Businessmen smoke whilst eating their toast and reading the papers. Rather suspiciously beautiful women hang out at nearby tables looking bored. I encourage the chef to make me some scrambled eggs and I find a stash of salmon on one of the tables. Washed down by cheap American-style coffee, it's a good start to the day.

Down in reception I study the crowd of people waiting to check out, and behind them near the revolving entrance door is my old Trans-Siberian friend and Muscovite fixer, Alexey. He's easy to spot: dressed in a woolly hat and duffel coat, he carries his papers in a brightly coloured plastic leatherette football bag just like one I had in the 1970s. It's so retro it looks a bit hip today. Shaking hands, I'm reminded of the cool Russian heart, but he's a nice guy and straight down to business, and he can't imagine that someone might like him so much that they would specifically request his services. 'Matthew, why are you here again? The office said you asked for me?' Sitting down in a coffee shop I explain each of the requests I have made to his HQ, though he doesn't believe them until I tell him myself. Finally, the old notebook comes out and he makes some notes. When I tell him not to bother with something on the itinerary from the office he insists that I sign a piece of paper indemnifying him from my rash decision. Agreeing on a plan for the day we head off into the snow-laden streets. The road crossing outside the hotel has a little green man with a hat on, but he only comes on for about 15 seconds every five minutes. A five-minute wait in this climate could prove fatal if you are under-dressed, so I hope our timing will be fortuitous this morning. Yesterday when I waited for that little green man my legs went red and needed reheating in the shower. But Alexey is onto this and times it perfectly. In just seconds we are down into the heated tunnels of the Moscow metro.

It feels a bit as if we are on a school outing. Alexey regularly checks on me, reminding me to be careful of things like pickpockets and the vicious metro turnstiles that could cut you in half if you haven't inserted your ticket correctly. I think he would hold my hand if he could, but social and legal convention would probably lead to our detention if he were to try. At first I have a view that this overwhelming duty of care for my safety is quite unRussian, but it's actually just another well-hidden national character trait.

Our first stop today is the Central Armed Forces Museum where I get to see the mangled U2 spy plane piloted by Gary Powers that was shot down over flying the Soviet Union in 1960. There isn't much of it left, but I'm pleased that Captain Powers was able to escape – only, rather sadly, to die in a helicopter crash in 1977. The wreckage is draped with rope lights and resembles a funfair accident. In the next room, past a seemingly endless display of subtly different Kalashnikov assault rifles, a further exhibit catches my eye. There is a large picture of a familiar enough-looking Trans-Siberian train, but there is something different about this one: the carriages have no windows. Alexey does some translation for me; the train has a special guest on board, an SS24 type Intercontinental Ballistic Missile. The missile has been specially shortened to fit into the carriage and at a distance this makes it indistinguishable from any other train. With a range of nearly 8,000 miles, the missile can be raised up and fired straight from the train. I make a mental note to avoid Trans-Siberian trains without windows.

In the afternoon we have a special appointment at Bunker 42, a place that until quite recently remained a classified Soviet secret. It was once a command and control centre for several thousand officials to live whilst the radiation from a nuclear holocaust subsided. The Soviets actually tested atomic weapons to find out the correct depth and building techniques needed for full protection. This bunker was constructed 65 metres beneath the surface, deep enough to survive a 15-kiloton warhead exploding overhead.

Our biggest challenge turns out not about being admitted, but just finding it. Walking down the streets of an anonymous suburb there are no signs, no clues to its whereabouts. Alexey thinks he knows where it should be from his map, and begins making a series of erratic turns until we finally reach a less subtle green-painted blast door with a little red star above a door within the door. What next? Will they spot us on a camera, or do we need to knock? Maybe there is a secret password involving an animal like a grey fox or even the state of the daffodils in Gorky Park. It turns out there is a buzzer and a Russian voice on an intercom. There is a quick exchange of words. I imagine Alexey said something like 'Excuse me, are we in the right place for the nuclear bunker?' I hear my name mentioned, the little door opens inwards to where a man dressed in a smart light green shirt and peaked cap motions us to come in quickly before someone sees us.

Inside we join a small group of tourists, each looking like they have won a golden ticket to Willy Wonka's chocolate factory – two Japanese girls, an Englishman in his 30s, an older German man and a Dutch couple. Before we can learn anything more of the secrets beneath our feet, the guard inspects my passport and Alexey's identity card. Once he confirms that we are on the list attached to his clipboard we can join the others.

Alexey selectively translates the short health and safety briefing, which is so dark it has comedic value – the most important final sentence being that we shouldn't press any buttons, as they may still be working. I hope the others speak either Russian or English, otherwise this might all go horribly wrong, and not in a Charlie and the Chocolate Factory sort of way.

Without too much time to think about the possibility of thermonuclear war, the guard leads us towards a nearby wall. He inserts his key into a control box and when he turns it, the wall slowly slides back to reveal that it is in fact an inner blast door, about two feet of solid concrete. It opens just enough for us to squeeze through the gap and carefully descend the 18 flights of metal stairs to reach the main tunnel that connects to the military area of the bunker. Catching my breath at the bottom, I see a view ahead of a weirdly carpeted tunnel sloping gently downwards towards a security post. Above us are overlapping metal plates bolted together like an ironclad ship, apparently to keep the radiation out.

After a short walk we emerge into the main control room. A vast open space with a high curved roof now above us, and on the floor below, banks of control desks complete with radios, radar screens and map plotters. Surely this is the set from a 1970s James Bond film? The one where the villain's base is hidden in a volcano and the roof slides back to let the spacecraft in.

We are free to wander around Ernst Blofeld's lair, and most of the others head off to a room where a man demonstrates the vintage military radios which cover the walls from floor to the ceiling. Trying to take in the atmosphere of the place, I choose to sit behind a wooden desk with just a red telephone, trying to imagine what might happen where it to ring.

Before I sink too deep in my thoughts, Alexey returns with some machine guns to play with. He hands me a new-looking assault rifle without explanation. It's an AK-74M. In his other hand he has a classic wooden-stocked AK-47 which he keeps for himself. An ex-conscript warrant officer, he's clearly highly proficient at checking the working parts are in order before making it safe. I on the other hand know nothing about how to make an AK-74 safe. The plastic moulded stock and folding butt are alien to me, so he helps me pull back the working parts and dry fire it. I could see that everything is real. All that are missing are the firing pin and the 5.45mm bullets in the iconic curved magazine.

Suddenly there is shouting behind us. We turn around to the slightly chilling sight of two wildly excited Japanese girls, now wearing helmets, trying to shoot each other with AK-47s whilst taking selfies. I decide to leave the other Willy Wonker winners to their fate, and head over to a selection of deactivated nuclear warheads at the far end of the hall.

Climbing up to a raised deck, the guide explains that this one was built for the release of nuclear weapons.

He asks for a volunteer to assist him in a practice missile firing exercise, and I can't seem to stop myself from thrusting my hand into the air and looking excited. Sitting behind a bank of monitors I'm even given a special hat to wear. This is pure *Doctor Strangelove*, and seems to go against the advice in the safety briefing not to touch anything. A sequence of buttons begins to flash on my desk and target locations appear on a huge map above us. I'm told to turn a key on his command and then enter a sort of Soviet PIN code into the ancient-looking computer keyboard. More lights blink and flash, and an occasional beep indicates the progress of the final countdown. I'm pleased to know of course that this console has been disconnected from the vast network of ICBM silos hidden across the Russian Federation. At least I hope it has.

Walking back towards a lift (why didn't they let us come down in the lift?), I can hear the rumble of nearby metro trains from beyond the tunnel walls. Heading back towards the surface, it looks like we are all still here, and I'm quietly relieved that the Japanese girls have changed out of their combat gear. In the reception area we bid the group farewell and head back out into the street. Down the road we pass a small group of tourists who look like they might be looking for the little green door, but I decide that it's not our job to divulge directions to Moscow's nuclear secret. Finding it is surely part of the admission test.

Back in Sokolniki that evening I enjoy a final stationery supper at a wonderful local Uzbek restaurant. Muscovites dress to impress, and this creates the challenge of surviving the low outside temperatures but still sitting down to dinner looking suitably elegant. The solution involves big boots and lots of what I assume to be real fur, and then to change at the restaurant. Nearly all of them have cloakrooms where you can deposit outdoor clothing before eating. I have no fur other than my ushanka hat, but I'm afraid to wear it for fear of being arrested for impersonating a senior naval commander. Instead I dive inside before my ears get frostbite and deposit just my down jacket. Normal trousers give you about ten minutes' protection before loss of circulation, so a big coat really would be more suitable here.

The manager finds me a menu in English and sits me at a low table near the kitchen where I'm happy to sip dark Russian beer and people watch. In front of me a slightly mad-looking friendly Uzbek man in a white dishdash bakes bread in a special oven. He smiles a lot to reveal some major gold reserves in his dentistry. Next to him is the man responsible for lighting and maintaining the brightly coloured glass hookahs. A smoking sommelier, he advises on tobacco flavours, and using his own special mouthpiece he gets each of his brews started off by lighting the charcoal and sucking air through the cooling water inside the glass before handing over control to the customer. Judging by the tips he is getting, this is an important skill in these parts. This evening I stick to beer to go with my delicious pilaf and grilled meat. There will be enough burning coal in the days ahead.

Day Seven, Moscow, Russian Federation
Distance travelled so far: 3,258 km

It has been a week since I left home, and I have pretty much forgotten about my normal life. It's too soon in my adventure to miss anything, and I have stopped worrying about my house flooding, or the late availability of organic turkeys in Waitrose. Today is my last chance to prepare for the one-week journey on the Trans-Mongolian train which I am embarking on tonight, so much of the morning is spent sourcing provisions and carefully packing them.

If you have never been to a modern-day Russian supermarket before, it's a much more exotic experience than you might imagine. I once visited an East German supermarket in the 1980s. The shelves were behind glass and counters were supervised by old ladies who scowled at you. First you had to pay for any item you wanted to buy and get a ticket, then return with the ticket to collect the item. The main problem for me in East Berlin on that day was not paying for something, but just finding something to buy, as one-way currency conversion was compulsory at the border. I ended up with some rather fine schnapps glasses. I wish I still had them as they would feel quite meaningful now. Some items don't seem important at the time, but become valuable once they have survived accidental disposal in an age that they are seemingly irrelevant or worthless.

The supermarket next to Sokolniki metro station isn't a glamorous one. If you seek the Moscow equivalent of Harrods, then you need to get on the metro and head south ten stops to the magnificent GUM department store. But even here in suburban Moscow, as soon as you are through the doors you can see how much things have changed. Despite the sanctions preventing the import of some foreign products, there is still a massive selection of local and imported food. Delicatessen counters with huge selections of fish, meat and cheese. Aisles devoted to selling tea, coffee and exotic booze and a hundred types of vodka. Not forgetting row upon row of more mundane items – Russian Pot Noodles, tins of apparently dead animals that you are not quite sure what they contain, and endless piles of packets of unusual crisps and snacks that have been fine-tuned to Russian taste.

Towing a plastic basket on wheels I manoeuvre my way methodically through the aisles. My shopping list is a bit vague in places, and I seek inspiration from the pictures on some items. I'm aiming for enough food to provide occasional breakfasts, lunch snacks and dinner on a couple of nights when we would be stuck in no man's land without a restaurant carriage. I settle on a Russian version of pot porridge for breakfasts, easy to make using water from the samovar. For snacks I fill my basket with savoury biscuits, cheese, cured sausage, packets of soup and tinned paté. For dinner my only real option is the humble Russian pot noodle and its cousin, the pot potato. Each one comes with amazing pictures of the feast that I would be creating by just adding hot water. Frankly if it looks like that, I'm surprised Gordon Ramsay or Marcus Wareing have not seized this as a gourmet trend. For treats I add bars of dark chocolate and packets of raisins. In the alcohol section I pass by the vodka aisle and try to find some suitable wine. I had imagined given the sanctions that this would need to come from Azerbaijan or maybe Bulgaria. But at the end of the aisle was a small mountain of Spanish plonk in one-litre cartons; unbreakable and easy to pack. The lady at the checkout knows straight away that she is dealing with a foreigner. I worry that I might mislead her into thinking that my purchases represent a normal diet for a Westerner. But whatever she thinks, she keeps her game face on and even helps me pack. What she might say to her co-workers once I have left, I have no idea.

The security man doesn't stop me but the staff look at me suspiciously as I cross the lobby of the hotel with all my shopping. Maybe they think I'm having a party. Safely in my room I unpack everything and lay it out on my big bed. Before leaving home, I read a book about rowing the Atlantic. Sailors usually chuck away bulky food packaging and use ziplock bags and sticky labels so they can organise and find things, and I had decided to take this approach too. I don't have to ration myself on the weight of things like a rower would – just their bulk, as two people need to be able to carry the bags. The bags I have chosen are hessian shopping bags with comfortable handles that I can carry okay, and then recycle as I consume my rations.

With the food sorted I sit at the little desk beside my bed and run a self-imposed admin session. When I used to play army games as a younger and more impressionable man, I had learned that the military know how to master paperwork. Whole days could be spent 'reviewing' paperwork, and it is a habit that for good or bad has stuck with me. For the trip I had set up a big folder with lots of plastic wallets inside. Each wallet contained tickets, timetables and printed copies of all the red tape sorted in chronological order. This made it easy to flip between legs of the trip and know where everything was. The next plastic wallet contained a pink airline-sized ticket that was proof of my Trans-Mongolian train booking. As it was printed in Russian, German and Chinese, I had little idea of its detail, but I could see that it was valid on carriage 11 of train 004 leaving tonight from Moscow bound for 'Peking'. Together with this I have an approximate timetable of the stops for the next few days and copies of my Mongolian and Chinese visas. All seems present and correct, so I zip it up and manage to fit it into a big camera bag that is acting as a mobile office.

Later in the evening I take a car down to Yaroslavski station to catch my train. The longer I spend in Moscow and use its metro the better I get at reading Cyrillic. At first it's just a seemingly meaningless jumble of odd-looking letters, then patterns begin to reveal themselves. As in an eyesight test, I get better at reading the names of places, and if I stare long enough I can deduce the odd word or two. The departures board inside the station is much easier than some of the signs in the metro. There are maybe ten trains on the board, and only one of them is headed for an international destination. The clues are there, 004, 21:35 and Peking – but I fail to find a platform number. Just as well I have Alexey with me, but I like to feel I could do this myself if the need arose. He leaves me in the warmth of the station hall where I sit surrounded by families with enormous quantities of luggage.

Although I don't know them and we have little in common, there seems to be an immediate politeness between my fellow travellers. People are thoughtful about finding space for new arrivals, and the lady behind me offers me a biscuit. But what I really fancy is a beer to mark a good stay in the city and to say farewell to my friend. But beer is nowhere to be seen in the station, so when Alexey returns I leave him looking after the modest pile of luggage and head out to find a liquor store. This is a scary experience, as once outside of the security provided by the soldiers and guards in the station, I am surrounded by mad people who have no intention of catching a train tonight. It must be a hard life living rough in this climate, not to mention the neighbours. Glad to make it safely back into the station, I am about to crack open an icy can of Baltika No 7, but Alexey says that it's not allowed inside the station building. Ever my protector, he lets me sip my beer surreptitiously from the can once it's inside a paper bag. It's probably best I get on the train before I get mistaken for a vagrant or worse.

At the appointed time we gather the bags and head outside to find the train. There are quite a few

Westerners hanging about by the departures board not sure where to go, but pretending not to be needing help. I smile and just say 'Peking?' Like a railway version of the Pied Piper of Hamelin, Alexey leads us into the snow. Heading sharp right and round the side of the main building, we see a platform for long-distance services. I can smell the smoke of the Chinese boilers well before I can see our train, but then there, under the dim glow of a few sodium lamps, are the dull green Chinese carriages of train 004. Carriage 9 is a short walk up from the back, and there to greet us is a guard with a torch and clipboard. Alexey helps me get all the bags off the platform and into the carriage where I do my best to remove the snow before it melts. We say our goodbyes, and he leaves me to my own devices. I will miss him hugely, but at the same time it's good to be back in command of my own destiny again.

Our train pulls out of Moscow Yaroslavski on time, at 21:35. For departing Russian trains the station plays stirring music and soldiers salute – but our Chinese train leaves without ceremony under the cover of darkness and light snow.

My carriage is one of two first-class soft Chinese sleeper carriages. Very decadent. I have been on this train once before. 'Soft' class is a Chinese description for the two-berth and four-berth compartments that come equipped with both beds and bedding. The four-berth compartments are very common and equate to *Kupe* on Russian trains. On this train, first class soft is called 'deluxe' by some ticket agents; each pair of two-berth compartments have a shared shower between them. This is a very unusual arrangement.

On my last trip this carriage was deserted and I was the only European passenger, but this time it is nearly full of Western tourists. Hearing their conversations is both comforting and mildly annoying at the same time. It's impossible to screen out their conversations, and I feel my experience is somehow less meaningful when shared by others. How antisocial and judgemental I must have become in a short space of time!

As is the norm with Chinese international trains, there are two guards to each carriage. Normally one is on duty and the other sleeping, but at big stops they are both up and on parade. They speak no English, and not knowing their real names I have adopted a protocol from a well-known Quentin Tarantino movie in naming them Mr Blonde and Mr Orange.

It takes me about an hour to sort my compartment out, make my bed and unpack. As I'm going to be here for a week it's worth getting everything out and storing things in the few little cupboards and spaces that I can find here. Getting things out of a big bag in a small compartment is a real pain, and the last thing you want to have to do with any regularity. There is enough room under the bed to slide my main bag under at one end, and I have a spare bunk that I can use to lay out useful items. At one end of this berth I have my outside gear, so whenever we arrive at a station I can quickly change and get off the train. My boots stay by the door, and I slip on some plastic sandals and a tracksuit, the uniform of any Russian Trans-Siberian traveller.

Tired from my busy day, I decide to forgo a trip to the restaurant carriage, and take an early night. Before turning in I take a wander down the carriage to inspect the toilet, and on the way I look in on several compartments occupied by tourists trying to make their bed or bemoaning what they have forgotten to pack. I shall try and help in the morning, but long-range rail adventure should really be about self-discovery, and I don't want to spoil anyone's experience.

My door has two locks, which I bolt shut before turning in. We will stop briefly at Nizhni Novgorod later tonight, a place that is rumoured to be slightly dodgy, so I want to be as secure as possible. I was given a tip that it's actually possible to open the locks with a knife from the outside, so I add an extra layer of protection with a cork which slides in behind one of the latches to make it more secure. No one is coming into my compartment tonight, and the motion is straight and smooth; snug in the wide and comfy lower bunk, I fall asleep in seconds.

Seven: Merry Christmas, Mr Blonde

Day Eight, Kirov, Russian Federation
Distance travelled so far: 4,210 km

Moscow time (GMT +3)

Station	Arrival	Departure
Vladimir	00:30	00:53
Nizhni Novgorod	03:40	03:52
Kirov	09:44	09:59
Balezino	13:27	13:50
Perm II	17:30	17:50
Ekaterinburg	23:10	23:33

We pull into Kirov at 09:36 this morning, bang on time. Wanting to get into the routine of life on the train as quickly as possible I take the opportunity to get off and stretch my legs. Down on the platform the crew are still wearing uniforms and caps rather than heavy coats and ushanka hats. Were it not for the freezing fog, it would probably be a nice day in Siberian terms. No one else gets off here that I can talk to, so with 20 minutes in hand I wander up to the locomotive by myself. I like to do this whenever I can. I'm not a trainspotter, but I feel it connects me with the train and I often get to exchange a few words with the driver, who for the next few days will be very Russian.

Another benefit of the walk is I can better understand the order of carriages – the DNA of our train. There is nothing worse than a six-carriage walk to find the restaurant carriage, when you discover that you have been walking in the wrong direction. At the moment our train is made up of a mix of Chinese coaches up front, including one with no windows that a paranoid passenger might mistake for a mobile ICBM launcher. I'm going to assume that it's a luggage van, though. Behind these are a couple of Russian coaches that will run as far as the Mongolian border, and between them, the distinctly older and shabbier-looking Russian restaurant carriage, the social centre of the train.

With no other appointments in my diary for today, I decide to reacquaint myself with the delights of a Russian Railways cooked breakfast. The journey to the restaurant carriage isn't so far and I'm used to hanging out and grabbing the frozen door handles between the carriages. There is a sense of anticipation and minor excitement about opening the final door. The restaurant carriage never matches the other rolling stock of the train. It's a random allocation, and its vintage, style and identity can vary enormously. It might have a Czech disco look, a rustic Russian style in wood and gold fittings, or even something I will describe as 'Siberian Modern', fitted out in bright plastic colours. Not only will the carriage vary in look but also in how it is run. I think the way it operates is as a soft franchise, usually with a husband and wife team and occasional helpers. They set the tone and ambiance, a little like a private club.

Pulling on the grimy door handle I'm greeted by the familiar smell of burned cooking oil and stale beer. The carriage is weirdly decorated with green plastic seats and lots of black metal in the style of some 1980s garden furniture. It is devoid of atmosphere or activity, other than Chef who emerges looking bleary-eyed and, perhaps uncharitably, pretty hung over. He hands me a thick plastic menu and returns with a little order pad and a big calculator with something taped to the top in Russian. A small dog senses the possibility of food and jumps out of a basket hidden under a nearby table, ready to follow him back in to the kitchen.

I opt for something I can recognise from the menu which is mostly translated into English, but with some occasional culinary twists. Fried eggs and ham arrive with fried onions and tomato sauce accompanied by a thick slice of stale brown bread. It might not be gourmet, but I'm pretty pleased with this, as I now know I won't have to depend fully on my own rations. There seem to be a range of options here for any time of the day, and everything is cooked to order.

An occasional Western traveller drops in for coffee, but strangely there are no Russian customers. I have a theory that the average passenger living in *plaskart* (third class) might rather spend the money on cigarettes and instant noodles, as it's not cheap compared to what things cost on the platform. Simple food and strong, thick coffee make me feel incredibly satisfied this morning.

The Trans-Mongolian isn't a particularly fast train, but by keeping moving all night and only halting for longer 20-minute stops perhaps half a dozen times each day it can cover a lot of ground, perhaps 1,000 km every 24 hours. Later in the day we rumble into Balezino, and as it the last daylight stop today I hop off to see what's going on.

Mr Blonde watches me carefully to see if I can be trusted with getting off at stops, especially as darkness approaches. On the platform the locals, living in plaskart at the back of the train, all chain smoke at the stops as smoking is no longer allowed on board. I stand nearby, stamping my feet and trying to look Russian. I get offered a lot of cigarettes, some black market vodka and a weird fish that smells like it might have been caught in the early summer. Up and down the platform there are mobile stalls selling everything from stuffed furry animals and local handicrafts through to essentials like Russian noodles and beer. To a Russian there is obviously nothing more normal than getting off the train to buy a pair of slippers and a suitable furry toy animal for their significant other.

Before getting back on the train I have a slightly alarming moment. Whilst I'm trying to determine the price of fish, the engine has uncoupled and a new locomotive arrives from the railway sheds of Balezino. There are no raised platforms as such, and in the nick of time I realise that I'm standing very close to the path of a train approaching from behind. How close isn't very clear, as several inches of snow has covered the tracks, but it's close enough that the driver sounds his horn and waves at me like I'm a village idiot. I look up at him in the cab of his huge red locomotive and don't have any signal to say I'm sorry. I read his expression as 'bloody tourists'. The fish woman acts like this happens every day, and continues trying to negotiate with me as the ground shakes and the train passes by just a couple of metres away from us. I need to be careful out here. Let's hope Mr Blonde didn't see that.

Back on board I fall into a routine of stops, meals, chats with other passengers and just watching the landscape change as we head east towards the Urals, our crossing point into Siberia. Today I'm listening to 'The Essential Collection' of Wishbone Ash, and hoping no one notices the occasional solo on my air drums. Life on board the train allows you to be as social or as private as you like. Some passengers leave their doors open and invite fellow travellers to join them for a game of cards or a meal, whilst others are hardly ever seen, just occasionally emerging to grab food from the platform. In my carriage most of the occupants are brave tourists, and gossip while making coffee at the samovar or sitting on the little pop-up seats in the corridor. Conversation so far is mainly about food, calculating the local time and whether the toilets are supposed to flush like that.

Late in the evening we pull into Ekaterinburg, right on time. It's an impressive station, befitting the large mining city known as the gateway to Siberia and a 'window to Asia'. It might be bedtime, but passengers are getting on and off this train at all hours of the day and night. Stations don't close: this is a 24-hour operation, driven by the carefully timetabled schedule of services crossing the continent. Under the dull yellow lights, figures move around in the shadows of stationary trains. Passengers don't hang around here for fear of freezing to the spot; rather they wait inside the station building and only head out onto the platform when they know there is a train waiting for them to get onto. Outside there is a soundtrack of announcements and the banging of metal bars on brakes. The sound of feet shuffling past on the crisp layer of frozen snow, and the occasional tractor passing to collect the mail or deliver supplies of coal. I fall asleep to the noises of platform life, which have already become familiar and strangely soporific.

Day Nine, Ishim, Russian Federation
Distance travelled so far: 5,683 km

Moscow time (GMT +3)

Station	Arrival	Departure
Tumen	03:54	04:14
Ishim	07:52	08:04
Omsk	11:24	11:40
Balabinsk	15:26	15:49
Novosibirsk	19:13	19:32
Taiga	22:35	22:37

I missed the morning briefing at daybreak. It's when

Mr Blonde and Mr Orange change shifts and update each other on all that has been going on over some freshly prepared dumplings in the little guard room next to where the corridor meets the outer doors. I have no idea what they actually talk about, but I think this is the time when they share views on their passengers and any major incidents. I can only hope that my name doesn't come up too often in the report.

My thermal blind snaps open when I release it. Ice crystals have spread right across the double-glazed window during the night. It's getting colder outside now and more bearable inside too – jungle training must be on hold. I don't have a thermometer, but this morning it's cold enough for the drain to my sink to be iced up. Outside is now a deep-frozen world where metal, coal and electricity fight with the force of nature.

As we approach Ishim my trusty Russian Railways pocket watch indicates that we are running half an hour late. This is unusual. The consensus amongst English speakers is that the brakes on our carriage have stopped working properly and we have had to slow down. Whenever the driver tries to brake the train, our carriage tries to do a full emergency stop. I'm hoping they can fix it this morning as it is throwing us passengers about a bit.

The locals on the platform at Ishim are dressed in big coats, fur hats and serious boots to cope with the climate. I like to think I can blend in with them when

I pull my ushanka on, but with the self-selected rank of something like admiral of the fleet, this is unrealistic. They stare at me for a few moments, before going back to their business of buying and selling things. Both Mr Blonde and Mr Orange are summoned by the man in charge to get to work on the underneath of the carriage, which has become clogged up with snow and ice. They poke about with steel bars as if cleaning the teeth of a metal monster. A man with an orange vest and an old-fashioned torch climbs under and inspects whatever is important down there. Whilst they sort the problem out I wander down towards the Russian carriages and the smokers. I thought our carriage was bad, but the exposed back entrance to one of their carriages has become completely filled with snow, and workers are busy with shovels tunnelling towards its blocked door. It's too cold to linger, so I climb the steps back into carriage 9 and shut the inner door behind me. From -20 to +30°C in just a few feet: I need to quickly get my outside gear off.

Once we are on the move I get some coffee on the go and try a Russian pot porridge whilst I listen to 'Can't Buy a Thrill' by Steely Dan as loud as I dare. The walls are not very thick, and next door have complained about my snoring in a polite way. The porridge tastes rather good and I wish I had brought more of these in Moscow as I have not seen any for sale on the platforms.

A whole new day lies ahead, and I have the luxury of nothing planned. I can choose to do nothing other than drink coffee and stare out the window, or choose to meet new people, explore unknown stations, write and read. We reach a white and wintry Omsk late in the morning where we repeat the three-times-a-day routine of a fresh engine with driver and a resupply of coal. This will see us through to this evening's stop at Novosibirsk. The locomotive is electric, but the coal heats the train and I imagine would be useful in keeping us alive if there were ever a power cut.

We are still getting accumulations of ice under the train that need clearing each time we stop. It is not just the brakes; the drains and the water tanks are also freezing up. The solution is to whack the bogies hard with a big metal rod to clear the ice, and then pour boiling water down the drainpipe.

There is another one of those suspicious-looking mail trains opposite us on platform 2. It is painted green and has no windows. On the platform soldiers appear to guard it, but I can see no obvious signs of missile-launching capability. On future Siberian adventures I will pack a geiger counter.

I treat myself to a cooked meal in Little Russia in the evening. Some rather good fresh salmon followed by a pork escalope washed down a couple of cans of Baltika No 7. The practical physics of keeping beer cold on a Siberian train are interesting. Given that it is now around -20°C outside, the beer fridge is actually keeping the beer warm. If you want cold beer you need simply to store it near the outer doors of the restaurant. That then leaves the problem of freezing, but with the alcohol it contains maybe it will not freeze until a point below absolute zero. Some further experiments are needed to determine what this freezing point is.

Getting off the train at Novosibirsk is perhaps the closest that I will ever get to feel what it is like taking a walk in outer space. With all my gear on, I grasp the metal rail that I would stick to were it not for my two pairs of gloves, and place my feet onto the frozen ground. Outside there is darkness, and taking a slow and careful walk up to the front of the train, total isolation. Just me and the driver in his illuminated cabin high above the platform. The engine looks enormous from the viewpoint of its front buffers. It gets changed at all major stops and I try to make it up to the front to say goodbye to the departing driver before he has uncoupled his engine, which normally takes less than five minutes. I then wait for the new loco to arrive and say hello to the new driver. They probably think I'm a trainspotter or a little bit mad. Come to think of it, I wonder if trainspotting might have been discouraged in the Soviet Union in case train numbers were secret. My spacewalk comes quickly to an end. I can't afford to risk being left behind here, so I begin the walk back down the platform.

To my untrained eye everything looks like it is working reasonably well in our carriage. The only visible sign of trouble is a minor flood in one of the compartments where the drain has frozen solid.

There are shared en-suite showers between each two compartments here in first class soft, but they would be better described as dribbles of lukewarm water from the end of a thin flexible pipe. Other than that, the toilet at one end of the corridor has frozen several times, but it responds well to a kettle of boiling water. I can see the design issue. The samovar that provides hot water and heating to the carriage is at one end, and the pipes that serve the toilet at the other end are maybe 20 metres away, so if no one flushes the toilet overnight or has a shower, the toilet freezes solid.

The engineer who lives on the train spends his day fixing problems like this, supervised by Mr Blonde or Mr Orange when attending to emergencies in our carriage. He normally arrives with a kettle, a massive spanner and a long piece of wire that looks like it has been made from a giant coat hanger.

This evening Mr Blonde is on duty. He seems to be the more communicative and fun-loving of the pair, and he smiles a lot. When Mr Orange is on duty he tends to do everything with vigour, but I can't help feel that he sees passengers as a distraction to his tasks like shovelling coal or de-icing the carriage. If you have ever seen the classic 1970s television series *Porridge*, then this is like comparing Mr Barrowclough with Mr Mackay.

The corridor is full of people supervising the plumber fixing our toilet again, so I retire to my compartment to perform a stocktake of my remaining rations. Four cartons pot porridge, two pot noodles, some tinned paté, sliced processed cheese and half-stale crackers. In the drinks cabinet I have four cartons of wine. I will need to find somewhere tomorrow to stock up, as the Russian restaurant will be leaving us well before the Mongolian border. I sometimes see the chef running off the platform at longer stops, and I suspect he knows a good place to shop quickly and make it back to the train before it leaves. Maybe I should follow him, but missing the train remains one of my greatest fears.

When the cost is clear and no one is watching I stash a carton of white rioja amongst the coal sacks at the end of the outer corridor to get it down to temperature. Mr Blonde sees everything, and introduces me to his private guard's fridge. There is just space for me to squeeze my wine inside amongst their provisions. It's kind of him to offer this space to me, and encouragement of the idea that if you are nice to people you nearly always get something back.

The guards take it in turns to cook their own food, and I don't think they would get on well with a Russian restaurant carriage diet. Their food looks much healthier and seems to consist mainly of stir-fried vegetables and dumplings washed down by large quantities of green tea. The good thing about storing my wine in their fridge is that it won't freeze there. The bad thing is it will take longer to cool than being left in the outer corridor. I have still to complete my experiment to discover the freezing point of wine that is 11 per cent alcohol by volume, assuming that it has not been illegally fortified with added antifreeze. I need some sort of chart, the reverse of one that tells you how long to cook something at a certain temperature.

Back in my compartment I have a tidy up, and restock my water bottles for the night ahead. First I fill my metal water bottle with boiling water from the samovar, let this cool and then dispense it into an old plastic mineral water bottle. The water is drinkable but has a unique taste that many would not find pleasant. I on the other hand, having gone slightly native, have decided that I quite like this.

My soundtrack for the evening is Pink Floyd's seminal 'Dark Side of the Moon', which seems rather appropriate for this place.

Day Ten, Krasnoyarsk, Russian Federation
Distance travelled so far: 7,457 km

Moscow time (GMT +3)

Station	Arrival	Departure
Krasnoyarsk	06:30	06:50
Ilanskaya	10:52	11:12
Nizhne-Udinsk	15:42	15:54
Zima	19:17	19:47
Irkutsk	23:25	23:50

I wake to a weird sensation inside my compartment. Outside I can hear crispy crunching sounds from people walking past on the station platform at Krasnoyarsk. Raising my window blind, I fall back on my bed with the sudden intensity of Siberian sunshine outside. It has stopped snowing.

A bit dazed by this I gather my wash bag and towel and head for the corridor, from which some strange sounds are emanating. Outside my compartment is Adam, a 20-something English passenger from next door but one, dressed in just a pair of shorts and trainers. He is performing some strange train-based aerobics.

'Er, good morning.'

'Morning, sir. Care to join me? It's going to be great fun; you get a sweat on in here, then head outside into the cold.'

'Perhaps I could just watch?'

In my book any activity that makes you sweaty in a place without a decent shower is madness. He looks like one of those soldiers on an arctic warfare course who is about to jump into a hole in the ice of a frozen lake. If you are wondering, the drill is to get out and roll in the snow to dry off before finding a blanket and a fire, otherwise your heart might stop. I saw that on the Discovery Channel.

Adam does a couple more squats and attempts a cartwheel in the narrow corridor before heading off to the outside world, leaving me to discover that the toilet door is of course locked, as we are in a station.

Plan B. Get off the train and see what's going on outside. It's pretty bracing, and if I had a cup of coffee I'm sure it would freeze if I threw the liquid into the air. There is no coal to load here for some reason. With no coal going on, there is also no indication of how close we are to departure so I decide to forgo my walk up to the engine and hang around our carriage. I try to take some arty photographs of the frozen train, but not of Adam, who is now pumping his muscles in all sorts of weird contortions on the platform. That would be a bit weird. Adam gives in to the vicious chill after about five minutes. I'm going to keep an eye on him in case he has hypothermia.

After a few minutes Mr Orange shouts down from the carriage and gesticulates that I'm to return immediately to the carriage. In spoken Chinese there is no perceptible difference to the foreigner between urgency and normal. Mr Orange might have simply been saying, 'Lovely view from this platform in the soft morning light. Have you tried F3.5 with a slightly longer exposure?' – but to me it sounds like 'Quick! Climb up now, fat foreigner, or you will be left behind in this icy cold place for ever!'

Time zones are constant problem for the Trans-Siberian traveller. Today I have made an executive decision and made the switch from Moscow time to Beijing time. This is a four-hour time change, but I feel I'm straddled between the two, and every day it gets more confusing, more tiring somehow. At least I will be anchored to my future rather than my past. Even though it is a Chinese train, the timetable is built around Moscow time and this does not change until the Mongolian border. However, the daylight –

and vitally the restaurant carriage, – operate in local time. A time that is not published anywhere, and I can only approximate by what people are up to. Even the clocks in the stations run on Moscow time. There is no perfect answer, but I have advanced my lifestyle to Beijing time, leaving one watch on Moscow time just so I can read the timetable properly. It's a bit more brutal than adding an hour each day, so I hope it works, as otherwise if I have got it wrong I might be having my lunch at breakfast time.

Time for some caffeine. As we clank across the bridge over the River Yenisei, I head down the carriage to perhaps the most important device on our train, the samovar. Like the Russian version, this Chinese one is a mass of steel pipes and gauges. Its instructions, however, are in Mandarin. At first I was a little intimidated by it, but now I know the most important things, like how to check the temperature, where the lever that turns it on and off is, and where the drain is for unwanted water. As I prepare my espresso machine, a small Russian boy materialises from a compartment and stares intently at what I'm up to. I show him how it works and he seems to understand it straightaway. He's amazingly confident and world-wise. He and his mother have recently joined the train and now live at the other end of the carriage. Breaking off from supervising my coffee making, he looks outside and tells me in perfect English, 'It's a beautiful forest.' It certainly is. It's probably just as well that he likes forests, as he lives in Krasnoyarsk, a place that must define the very meaning of being in the middle of absolutely nowhere.

I take my breakfast later than usual today, as last night there was a rumour that some caviar might be on the menu. After a couple of glasses of quite reasonable red wine from Azerbaijan, I managed to make a communication breakthrough with the woman who runs the restaurant. After several days living on fried eggs and stale bread rolls, I hear that caviar and salmon might be on offer this morning. Or was this all actually just a twisted dream sent to my brain by my digestive system?

I shuffle purposefully down the train towards the restaurant carriage, hoping that I have worked out the right time for breakfast. Opening the final door, I'm greeted by a tired-looking chef. This is hopefully a sign of overnight fish trading on icy station platforms rather than a big night out. The curtains are still drawn, almost as though this needs to be a well-guarded secret. Two police officers hang around for some time talking to passing passengers, but I have no idea what is being said. Are they guarding the fish, or even on the lookout for any black market caviar smugglers? Eventually the policemen leave and the woman who takes the orders approaches and guesses what I'm after. The caviar comes with pancakes and garlic butter, but the salmon has either already gone or didn't make it on board. The pancakes taste simply heavenly, and cost me just 290 roubles, about £3.

The sunny morning flies by to my soundtrack of 'Hunky Dory' and 'Scary Monsters' by David Bowie. The climate has changed over the last day or two. There is a little less moisture around now, less snow. I have the map out on my chart table – well actually, it's just a table, and I drink cups of steaming coffee whilst listening to the back catalogue of the Electric Light Orchestra. I have always wondered what Jeff Lynne looks like without sunglasses, but suspect he might even wear them in bed. The map suggests that we might have gained some altitude by reaching a plateau on the way east and slightly south towards Lake Baikal.

In my calendar it will be Christmas Eve tomorrow, so I put up a few decorations that I have brought along with me. I have some tinsel to go around the window which, if I say so myself, rather nicely frames the outside world, some illuminated stick-on snowflakes, and best of all a mini Christmas tree that I plant on my table. It has flashing LED lights which will look superb after dark. All that I need to do now is to play some Christmassy music and to cook the Christmas pudding that I have been carrying in my bag for the occasion.

We make an afternoon stop in Ilanskaya for coal. My train timetable says that we are now 4,379 km from Moscow, so if I covered 1,502 km getting to Moscow, then that's 5,881 km in the bag so far, further than I had guessed. There is lots of platform food action here. Traders gather outside the carriage doors. They are selling particular items, rather than the kiosks which have been selling everything. Outside our carriage I spot dumplings, honey, hooch, and dried fish. The mode of transport for these mobile shops is by sledge between the platforms. There is even a man selling coffee beans, but I have neglected to pack a grinder. How remiss of me.

One of the plaskart carriages toward the back of the train has been full of hidden soldiers, now busy loading a lot of gear down onto the platform. It looks like they are going camping. I can't work out if this is basic Russian outward-bound survival or special forces training, but it is definitely cold enough to guarantee ice in your mess tins, even in the daytime. Rather them than me.

As I'm out and about on the platform I supervise the attachment of the new locomotive and wave at the driver. He waves back from the cab of his pale blue engine. It looks quite a bit older than the one it has replaced. Mr Orange is standing back from the carriage and probably looking for me, so I walk back, taking in the direct sun on my face before climbing back aboard.

I spend a relaxed afternoon chatting to fellow passengers about their plans. There are a couple of Londoners next door getting off in Irkutsk tonight – that's about midnight train time, but locally in time for breakfast and with limited chance of sleep. I wish I was stopping here too, but at this stage of the journey I feel the need to keep moving.

Adam pops by for a chat too. Like me, he is heading for Singapore, but he plans to take a bus route south through Laos. He's got a new job and is carrying pretty much just a suit, a couple of shirts and a tie. He suggests that I invest in some hostage insurance for my trips, and gives me a contact in London. His father is the chairman of a well-known shipping company who is keen not to have to pay a ransom if his number one son is taken hostage. Oh, good. Something new to worry about.

My Beijing time zone says it's not long until beer o'clock, so I get ready to put on my gloves and head torch for the journey backwards four carriages to the restaurant I know as Little Russia. Getting between carriages is a skill that I seem to be getting quite good at. The trick is never to let go of the door handle of the carriage you are leaving until you have the next handle in your hand. Does that sound like an ancient Chinese proverb? It should be. The only flaw in my technique is the snow and ice penetrating my plastic slippers and freezing my toes, but it's not the done thing to wear your outdoor boots once inside the train. Mr Blonde even lays out a carpet cover in the corridor when it snows, to protect it from boarding passengers.

Late each evening after the last big stop of the evening one of the guards shuts up our inner carriage doors and pulls down the thermal blinds covering each of the windows in the corridor. By this time most people have turned in for the night, but this evening I am still reading my book (*Chickenhawk*,

Robert Mason) and enjoying a glass of rioja with my door open in case anyone drops by for a chat. Mr Blonde looks in on me and notices my Christmas decorations twinkling in the semi-darkness. He thinks about this for a bit, before wishing me a 'Happy New Year'. But he's back five minutes later with a gaggle of guards from other carriages to show them the farang with the Christmas lights. I think they all approve, and I wish them all a Happy Christmas before finally shutting my door as I was beginning to feel like a reluctant animal in a zoo.

Day Eleven, Ulan-Ude, Russian Federation
Distance travelled so far: 8,948 km

Moscow time (GMT +3)

Station	Arrival	Departure
Ulan-Ude	07:27	08:04
Dzida	12:08	12:10
Naushki	13:08	16:43
Dozorne	16:54	16:57

Ulaanbaatar time (GMT+8)

Suhe-Bator	21:30	23:15

It's another day of sunshine, and a new landscape. I didn't get up to say goodbye to people getting off in Irkutsk, and I feel like I have had some good sleep. I must have drunk too much coffee, and I am playing various air guitars and drums to some vintage Fleetwood Mac in the privacy of my compartment before breakfast.

We seem to be about half an hour behind schedule and I factor this into my calculation for the stops ahead today. The train has been weaving around Lake Baikal overnight. By chance I was walking back from my ablutions after dawn and I nearly dropped my toilet roll when I looked out the window in the corridor to see the lake for the first time. It is absolutely massive, stunning, like a sea, but at this time of year completely frozen. It's mostly hidden by a forest along its banks, but from time to time the track passes right by the edge of the lake, where you can look out past frozen waves at the shoreline towards a vanishing point on the horizon of empty frozen lake.

Idly strolling through the corridor of the carriage provides me with a real slice of Trans-Siberian life. Posh backpackers sharing travel ideas over instant noodles, Mongolians mainly sleeping, Russians watching violent soaps on old laptops, and Chinese guards cooking fresh dumplings in the fire of the samovar.

A minor disaster was narrowly averted last night. My Dutch neighbours, with whom I share the space that some glamorously describe as a bathroom, managed to leave the shower on before they got off at Irkutsk. I know how this can play out as yesterday my neighbours on the other side of me had a flooded compartment when someone had an overly long shower. It turns out that I have been quite lucky. What has saved me from a watery compartment is that the shower was left on in the hot position, so the water in the drain didn't actually freeze. Let's hope we have enough water left until next resupply. I don't know much about how much water we carry and how often it gets replenished.

The samovar won't boil this morning, but I think that's an unrelated problem. Mr Blonde says simply 'later' when I ask him about some hot water for my morning fix of reasonable coffee. I don't know if he means it will be fixed in a few minutes or a few days, but that's a bit odd, given we are burning tonnes of coal each day to keep the carriage at jungle temperature.

Ulan-Ude is a significant stop on the Trans-Siberian railway. It is the last stop before the line splits in two, with a route onward east to Vladivostok, and a track headed south-east towards Mongolia and the Gobi Desert. The station is busy and there are two or three big trains being worked on by the station staff. It feels lovely to be in the sunshine, but I think it's all in the mind; the temperature is seriously cold, so cold in fact that I decide to deploy the ear flaps of my ushanka and tie them under my chin. When someone back home describes the weather as 'freezing outside' they need to come here to recalibrate. Below -20°C I have started to view the temperature as just a number. Having dropped to -35°C the other night, it's not fundamentally different, other than perhaps more painful to breathe the dry super-chilled air.

I have begun to notice that people look a bit different here, not so much European, more Eurasian. Their skin is darker and they have rounder faces. They smile more too. Despite the temperature today everyone except Mr Orange seems in good humour. But Mr Orange isn't a humorous person. He shovels coal and keeps his game face on.

There is a new phenomenon on the platform. Mongolian traders have appeared and they have great piles of wooden boxes containing eggs, fruit, vegetables, nuts and probably black market contraband. Ulan-Ude is the trading gateway to Mongolia, the first and last major stop on the Russian side of the border. I keep a close eye on their activities, as I heard that they tend to stash boxes in every available space on the train, even in compartments that they are not inhabiting. The quantities of goods are huge given that this is essentially hand luggage. I'm sure that any low-cost airline chief executive would have a nervous breakdown if they travelled on this train.

Whilst the Mongolians form human chains to pass the boxes onto the plaskart carriages, the coal truck makes its way down the train, stopping at each carriage to refuel. This is taking longer today as the guards are filing extra sacks and leaving them in the frozen outer corridor of the carriages. I assume that this is because the distance and remoteness of the next two days puts extra pressure on the supply chain, and running out of coal could be quite serious.

Once a fresh engine is hooked up, it's all aboard and we say goodbye to Ulan-Ude. To begin with the journey involves criss-crossing the river valley that spreads out into a wide flood plain. Then a new sensation that I have not felt for several days; we are climbing uphill, gently at first but then more steeply, and the train is noticeably slower. Once free of the valley we skirt round increasingly significant hills, in turn hiding even bigger hills behind them. By the middle of the afternoon we reach a height where there are no more trees, then not even grass, just thin topsoil. This is the edge of the Gobi Desert. After several days of nothing but trees and snow, it's intriguing to see just flat open ground on the plateau.

It is time to pay my final visit to the restaurant carriage, which will not be coming over the border tonight. I enjoy a Kozel beer and chat about border protocols with a couple of Mongolians. It sounds like it might be a long night ahead.

At 16:54 Moscow time the train pulls into Dozorne right on time. This is the Russian frontier station with Mongolia. The engine is uncoupled and it switches tracks to reappear at the back of the train and retrieve the few Russian carriages, and vitally the restaurant carriage. I hope everyone is in the right portion of the train now. Blowing its horn to say farewell, the engine heads back in the direction of Ulan-Ude. It is just about still light here, and out of the door I can see that all that remains of the train are seven Chinese first- and second-class sleepers and the 'mail van', or mobile ICBM launcher, depending on your level of paranoia. We are very much alone in this station, surely one of the most remote in the world, perched on the very edge of the desert.

At first Mr Orange says I have to stay in the carriage, but then Mr Blonde overrules him and tells me I can get off, but must stay nearby. It's too cold to linger outside and there is nothing to see on the platform other than a sign in English, Russian and Chinese that suggests almost certain imprisonment to anyone who crosses the line that marks the end of the Russian Federation and the no man's land before Mongolia.

The samovars keep the carriages warm and we wait for the process of migration to begin as the sun turns briefly purple in the dry sand-filled sky. I get out my file, fill in the paperwork that I have been given and wait. I have found that the trick with these border crossings is just to continue as normal. Recognise that you are not in control of the speed of the process, but you can choose how to spend your time. I choose to spend my time watching *Spies Like Us* on my tablet and eat what is thankfully my last Russian pot noodle. The pictures on the outside of the packet bear no resemblance to its contents. The film is cracking, and the perfect antidote to crossing the border. It wasn't very popular when it was released in 1985, but has something of a cult following these days, and I can see why. I laughed so much I gave myself hiccups at one point. I don't think it would be very popular with Soviet security officials as it might be seen to be a bit too close to the reality of the launch of a mobile ICBM. I would go as far as to guess that Warner Brothers have never found the need to provide a version of the DVD with Russian subtitles.

You can hear them coming, long before you see

them. Boots marching in almost perfect time and the slamming of carriage doors up and down the train mean that it is only moments before the interrogations will begin. I try not to tense, just to look relaxed: I'm not the droid they are looking for. What do you call a collective group of immigration officials? A gaggle? A mob? A troupe?

It is quite hard to work out the jobs of the different people who visit me over the next couple of hours. The main jobs are to de-register my Russian visa and check I'm not smuggling anything into Mongolia. The first immigration man who visits me gets to work on the paperwork with vigour. He carries a leather case which contains a complete set of passport stamps to cover any eventuality. I'm hoping he will just need the regular exit one for me. He seems happy enough for a Russian border official, and leaves with my passport and paperwork once he is sure I'm the person I'm claiming to be. Maybe he's going to check me out some more on a computer. Next to visit our carriage is a single soldier who comes through with a big dog. I don't think it's a pet, so it's there to either intimidate us or to sniff for drugs. Maybe both. I'm a little relieved when he walks past my compartment without any pause. The next stage of the procedure is a DIY lesson. A man with a power screwdriver and a step ladder appears. He is literally taking the carriage apart to search for anything hidden. Working his way through each compartment, he removes the ceiling panels one by one and checks behind them. When he is satisfied that the voids are empty, he re-attaches them and seals them with marking tape. By the time he reaches my HQ he hasn't made any big finds, and his search of my compartment is perhaps more cursory than some of the others.

As fast as they have come they leave us again. Silence. Just the hum of some emergency power for our dimmed carriage lights. The Mongolian railway is diesel powered and we are without any engine to generate power. Just coal for the boiler, and I assume a back-up battery for the lights. I go back to watching my film until the man with the briefcase returns with my passport. He gives me a curt salute before marching off down the corridor.

There is an unexpected jolt as a kinetic wave sweeps down the carriages and knocks over both my glass of wine and remnants of my meal. Bugger. A new engine has just connected with us, not gently, but more like at ramming speed. There is obviously no structural damage though, as soon we are powered up and heading off over the border to the Mongolian frontier station at Suhe-Bator. It has taken two hours to get this far, and the schedule, now in local time, suggests we are about half way through the border process. As well as a few officials still on board the train, there also seem to be a few not-so-officials. I think these people are black market currency traders, offering local torag at a rate far better than in any bank. I hear that the new train restaurant carriage will accept torag, roubles, and even US dollars, so I'm not doing any currency dealing tonight.

We repeat the paperwork process again, this time with officers wearing Mongolian badges on their hats. Immigration seems slightly more relaxed than on the other side of the border, but the Customs people are having a field day up and down the train with the traders. I seem to pass my first inspection, which includes a full bag search, but then a lady soldier dressed in full combats and boots returns to my compartment with a dog and a flashlight. I can only hope she is not on the lookout for a bin end parcel of cheap Spanish wine.

At just before midnight we get the all clear and the newly configured train sets off in the direction of Ulaanbaatar, Ulan-Bator, or just UB. Outside I can just make out the silhouette of farm buildings in the darkness, the train tracks having to snake around the territorial mud walls of their wild-dog-infested paddocks. After getting used to a straight track all the way through Siberia these curves and bends seem unusual at first. I check my watch and make plans to rise early for the stop in UB early in the morning. Before turning in I lock both my compartment door in both places and then the shower room door in case new travellers occupy next door during the night. Lights out at 00:15 and almost immediate slumber.

Eight: The Kamikaze Train

Day Twelve, Ulaanbaatar, Mongolia
Distance travelled so far: 9,533 km

UB time (GMT +8)

Station	Arrival	Departure
Ulaanbaatar	06:30	07:15
Choyr	11:33	11:53
Sain-Shanda	15:06	15:43
Dzamynude	19:10	20:35

Beijing time (GMT+8)

Erlian	21:00	00:57

I've made a point of getting up early for our arrival into Mongolia's capital city. It is 06:30 Beijing time and still quite dark outside and the temperature is somewhere in the -30s. Despite this the platform is buzzing with locals carrying quantities of parcels wrapped in brown paper. They mix with Western tourists who wear serious-looking rucksacks and insulated climbing boots. UB is the starting point for much of the Mongolian winter sports business, and a few brave souls are leaving the warmth of the train to live in a *ger* (a Mongolian yurt) and fish for their supper through holes in the ice.

117

In my delicate state it's both too early and too cold to get off the train, so I lurk in my bedclothes at the end of the corridor and carefully sip the freezing Mongolian air together with Mr Orange. He wouldn't like me to describe myself to you as hanging out with him, but after a few days in the same carriage he tolerates me being in the same vicinity as long as I don't get in his way. From my vantage point I can make out coloured disco lights from a place around the back of the station building; the party must still be in full swing. A door round the side says just 'VIP'. This is clearly the Mongolian equivalent of Kings Cross.

The only passenger joining our carriage here is a single lady who is helped aboard by three men to carry all her bags. I don't think she is Mongolian, as I would expect the locals to use their own native first-class carriage, so maybe she is Chinese. The train is now made up of several Mongolian sleeper cars where the Russian carriages used to be, a new restaurant carriage and the original Chinese carriages towards the front, together with the ICBM launcher behind the engines. One locomotive in Russia has become two in Mongolia, and these are changed here in UB. Our new locomotives have just tooted at us as they pass by on the next track – a pair of colourful diesels to power us across the Gobi.

I spot Mr Blonde emerging from the guards' day cabin and wish him a good morning. Our conversations are short but always friendly. He has the comforting habit of repeating some of the words that I have just said. Our conversation this morning is as usual focused on the English obsession with the weather. I'm going to need to start throwing some open questions in as he says 'yes' to a lot of things when he might mean 'no'. Our conversations often go along the lines of 'How long is this stop?' to which he thinks a bit and then says 'Yes.' 'Twenty minutes?' I add holding up lots of fingers. 'Yes,' he proclaims. Oh, that's all clear then.

Today Mr Orange is standing in the doorway and assessing people as potential first-class soft material. He won't let anyone up the steps without a close inspection of their tickets first. Although several purport to be soft class passengers their paperwork is not in order, so he shoos them off and points to the Mongolian carriages down the train with a firm but self-satisfied expression. I bet China Railway have a whole day course practising passenger scenarios like this one.

We have only three stops today, the final one being the Chinese border in the early evening. Jungle training continues on board the train as Mr Orange shovels fresh coal into our fire throughout the day. I notice for the first time that he has a standby electric heater that he switches on in the stations – the fire tends to fill the carriage with smoke unless we are moving forwards.

Retreating to my compartment I do the decadent first-class soft passenger thing of going back to my bed to warm up. My body clock is all over the place.

My stomach is in Moscow, and my head is in Novosibirsk, but none of me is yet in the time zone of Ulaanbaatar.

On the table next to my head when I lie in my bed is an unopened Russian pot porridge. In the interests of science, I am conducting a small experiment here in my compartment. The porridge is providing me with a basic indication of barometric pressure. It has come from Moscow unopened and is now ready to burst. We are over 1,200 metres higher here, not including any effects of weather. I'm planning to eat it for my breakfast tomorrow as I fear I may otherwise become victim to an oat-and-strawberry-infused IED exploding at close quarters to my head. I plan to open it at the end of the corridor and point it out the door.

I really need a strong cup of coffee to get going, but there is once again no hot water in our carriage. Asking Mr Blonde when the samovar will be working, he says, predictably, 'Later.' This isn't an indication of any urgency in my experience so far, so I'm not holding my breath. Despite the lack of caffeine, I enjoy watching our progress crossing into the desert to the soundtrack of Pink Floyd's seminal 'Wish You Were Here' turned up quite loud.

I pull myself together for the next stop at Choyr, a place most famous for the fact that it was home to Mongolia's first ever cosmonaut, Major General Jügderdemidiin Gurragchaa. After 124 successful orbits, he returned to Earth on 30th March 1981, strapped into the tiny capsule of the two-man Salyut

6. There is a monument to Mongolia's 'rocket man' at the back of the station.

Taking in the sunshine I head up and see what a Mongolian locomotive looks like. I try to trick my brain that it's warm in the sun, but my bones and exposed flesh are on the edge of mutiny. Deciding to keep moving, I make it to the front of the train in a few minutes and it's well worth it. Gleaming in the sun are two silver engines adorned with Mongolian writing and symbols that look like nothing I have seen before.

I meet many interesting people at the front of trains. Most are trainspotting travellers like me, there to take that gratuitous picture of themselves with the engine. Some are men in coats with big glasses and a little notebook, but most are just ordinary travellers after a memorable photograph to share with their friends. They tend to chance the walk up to the front of the train in the daylight and don't hang about here for fear of being left behind. This morning though I seem to be the only passenger keen enough to make the journey.

I'm alone until a distinctively dressed Mongolian man walks across the tracks and stands next to me on the platform, looking up at the new engines. I can't help but admire his outfit, a sort of bright blue tailored suit, red cravat, big sunglasses and flying boots, topped off with a soft cap. He carries a swagger stick with a silver tip in one hand and a small briefcase in the other. If this man is a trainspotter, then trainspotting must be a very hip pastime in this country.

We don't exchange many words, but as fellow train enthusiasts, we savour the moment and admire the train together. I ask him if he will take my photograph, which he does with apparent delight. He must be feeling the cold too. When he hands back my camera he tells me he has to go. We shake hands before he heads off down the platform and I watch him walk down to the end of the second engine, and then rather alarmingly, climb up onto it. Does he know that this isn't allowed? Trainspotters belong on the platform – or are there different rules here in Mongolia? Then the penny drops; he's the new driver.

He looks too well-dressed to be a train driver, but maybe in this country this is like being the pilot of a Concorde. He is after all piloting the legendary Trans-Mongolian. His salary might include an allowance for tailored flying suits and silver-tipped tools. I watch as he completes a series of pre-departure checks of the train, adjusting blinds, tapping things with his stick and settling into a seat at the front of the thousands of tonnes of heavy metal that he now commands. He smiles and waves at me from high above, and I return a faux Russian salute before retreating back towards carriage 9, where I decide not to tell the others that our train is now being driven by a well-dressed driver with the look of a posh kamikaze pilot.

Mr Blonde has been keeping an eye on me from further down the platform. I'm assuming that he gets marked down in his appraisal if he leaves any passengers behind. He's a lovely chap, really kind to us foreigners. Pleased to see me back outside carriage 9, he suggests getting on board in gentle sign language. He doesn't have to ask me twice. My spacewalk for today is complete. I'm frozen.

There is some excitement on board our carriage. My next door neighbours have just returned from the new Mongolian restaurant carriage and are describing it in detail to fellow passengers. Totally different from the Russian one, it has an interior carved of ornate wood and is covered with ancient musical instruments and weapons of long past wars. Were there to be a competition for the most amazing restaurant railway carriage in the world, this one would be in the top five. But those above it would be on luxurious private trains. This is an everyday scheduled service.

Somewhat euphoric from the cold and my encounter with the driver, I head two carriages forward and find the restaurant in its new position, closer to my home. It is indeed a magical place. My table is covered by a fresh yellow tablecloth and shiny metal cutlery. My icy Golden Gobi beer arrives in a branded glass and tastes fantastic. I decide to try some dumpling soup, which after a diet of fried Russian food, tastes just superb. The excitement of new food, new beer and a new landscape puts me in a wonderful mood. The scenery outside is equally interesting after the forests of Siberia. We pass endless telegraph poles and the occasional farmer on a motorbike chasing their camels. This is a bit like the famous view that Basil Fawlty tells Mrs Richards about. All that is missing are, unsurprisingly, the herds of wildebeest sweeping majestically across the plain.

Crossing Mongolia by train only takes a single day, and the time just whizzes by. The Western travellers can't get enough of the restaurant and its eclectic menu of local dishes. The place is crowded most of the day, as the manager says they are being uncoupled at 7pm and everyone wants both lunch and dinner before we cease to have any catering until China. I return later and try their Travelers Beef which is not only excellent, but comes with a little decorative garnish on a branded plate. Not having seen a garnish since leaving home, I'm pretty impressed.

The Trans-Mongolian rolls into Dzamynude in the early evening, having said goodbye to the lovely Mongolian restaurant manager. I had imagined a comedy farewell, jumping across the gap and waving at the detached carriage from an open door as we clatter onwards. In reality, the fear of being in the wrong part of the train when it was split up drove me back to my compartment quite early. Waiting for me at my table is a small pile of new paperwork to complete.

Soldiers salute the train as it arrives on the platform, heralding several hours of searches and inspections. Déjà vu? I have filled in the paperwork for both sides already, so hopefully I'm ahead of the game tonight. The Mongolian border officers seem to be almost exclusively female and to me they all appear stunningly attractive. They pass my compartment in small groups, some even holding hands. Maybe I have been on the train for too long.

During our first Customs inspection my passport is viewed with some suspicion. I have to explain that the United Kingdom is in fact almost the same as Great Britain, and that makes me British. Instantly satisfied with this explanation, the inspector moves on to the next compartment. The process on this side of the border is quite short and smooth compared to last night, but it still takes ages to search the train.

Two hours later, we make a short trip across no man's land to Erlian on the Chinese side of the frontier where music, lights, guards, and much impressive marching greets the train. Soothing music echoes around the platform, mainly 'Greensleeves', along with the less peaceful cacophony of slamming train doors. The carriage is suddenly flooded with very businesslike Chinese officials admiring my Christmas lights, but trying not to be noticed doing so.

With the paperwork and searches completed Mr Blonde says I can get off the train before we leave for the sheds to change wheels. But with no understanding of when I might be able to get back on again, I choose to stay with my belongings in the warmth of carriage 9. Most of the Mongolians get off, and I wonder if I have made the right decision. The shunting process proves to be quite destructive to anything not well packed and in a bag on the floor. Each time the shunter arrives to take off another carriage it smashes into the train. After ten minutes, all of my belongings are scattered across the floor of my compartment, where I leave them until the train is reassembled. I carefully hang on to my glass of rioja, but even this gets spilled if I don't correctly judge the timing of the impact. The process is the opposite of what we went through back in Terespol, as the wheels and bogies are now swapped from the broader Russian gauge to the standard gauge used in most of the world. Once lowered onto the Chinese bogies and reconnected to form the train, we return to the platform to collect the passengers who got off. They look deeply chilled and not in a happy way. They have had nearly three hours in a waiting room with a shop just selling packets of noodles and weird sweets. The soldiers stand to attention and salute the train as we slip out into the darkness, bound for Datong and hopefully Beijing tomorrow lunchtime.

Day Thirteen, Datong, China
Distance travelled so far: 10,400 km

Beijing time (GMT +8)

Station	Arrival	Departure
Datong	07:59	08:11
Zhangjiakou	10:36	10:46
Beijing	14:04	

The Trans-Mongolian spends just 14 hours in China before arriving at its final destination, Beijing, or Peking as I'm reminded on my ticket.

I think I'm becoming obsessed with food. Partly the excitement of changing cuisine as a proxy for geographical progress, and partly just out of boredom. Meals are part of my daily routine, and without them I fear I might not get out of bed some days. There is a fresh wind from the east on the catering front today. It's no longer possible to just arrive at the restaurant carriage when you fancy, as there are now closely prescribed times for meals. I have a little white ticket that I need to hand in, and it has the times I'm expected written on it. As I have two berths, I'm given two tickets, and I wonder who I might be able to invite to join me as my guest. Breakfast is set as 06:30 to 07:30, an impossibly early time for me, so I miss it all together. Even more bizarrely lunch starts at 10:30 and finishes just an hour later. I think part of this is down to the attitude of the Chinese staff, who like to congregate, drink tea and smoke in the restaurant like it is some sort of works canteen. They won't even let you in outside of the official times. There is no menu as such, but it is

127

all quite friendly and efficient, as long as you arrive on time and with the right coupon.

The layout of the new restaurant carriage is quite different from the ones in Russia and Mongolia. From the end I arrive in there is a rather grubby mop-and-bucket-filled corridor past the kitchen, and then an open servery looking out of the kitchen so you can see the chefs at work. At the entrance to the restaurant itself there is a welcome addition: a locked cabinet with glass doors containing bottles of China Railway red and white wine. Their brand is called Great Wall, but sadly there will be no time to arrange a tasting today. Before reaching the tables, there is a desk where you get checked in, and as seems to be normal in a Chinese train restaurant, a policeman is on hand to prevent possible noodle theft and black market exchanges of meal coupons. My brunch today is a bit bland, but slightly adventurous as chopsticks are now provided. Plain rice, stir-fried cabbage and an unidentifiable meat-based dish is served with lashings of tea, the kind that has loose leaves in the glass. It isn't a place to linger, so I quickly retreat after eating my first and last Chinese meal on this train.

The scenery has changed dramatically since the sun set at Dzamynude last night. Now in Inner Mongolia, a province of China, the railway line passes through massive gorges with frozen rivers and tunnels cut through the final mountain range between us and Beijing. These are the only tunnels on the entire journey from Moscow, and the sensation of sunshine to darkness every few minutes takes some adaptation.

With the lights turned on in my compartment I begin to pack up my gear. I'm determined not to leave anything behind, and this means making sure I remember all the little hiding places I have found to store things over the past week.

Once I've packed I have little to do, and my routine is stunted by the lack of stops and no access to a restaurant. As the mountains open up to plains and the farming encampments are replaced by factories, I reflect on the journey so far. I have covered just over half the distance of my mission in just 13 days. It will take much longer and become more intricate as I proceed beyond Beijing. The cumulative effect of two weeks on the move in the cold outside and the unrelenting heat on board the train has left me a bit shell-shocked, and I need some rest and recuperation to get myself into shape for my next tour of duty: I'm bound for Vietnam next, on the twice-weekly express service from Beijing to Hanoi via Nanning.

Beijing's central railway station is an enormous concrete bunker, but its design is quite open plan, and in some ways has a European feel. There are no real barriers, and it is relatively easy to find your way around compared to the other stations in the city which run a more confusing system of waiting rooms and gates. There is an end-of-term feel in our carriage, and as the guards collect bedding, travellers are packing and exchanging contact details. The corridor gets its first clean with a mop since I moved into my compartment. Looking round, I think I will miss this carriage. I have had the luxury of my own space for an extended period. For the rest of the journey I will be sharing my accommodation with other travellers. I'm paranoid that I have left something behind, so search around several times to find hidden treasure. The only treasure I have deliberately left behind are a couple of Russian Pot Potato meals.

I say my farewells to the passengers I know and wish Mr Blonde and Mr Orange well. I give them each a small bottle of Scotch to thank them for keeping me alive in the depths of the Siberian winter, and even Mr Orange looks pleased with that. I wonder if he is a bit of a Jekyll and Hyde-type character, and lets his hair down once he gets home. I shall never know.

The train looks rather sad now without its passengers. I take one final walk up to the front, where a single dark blue Chinese electric engine is still attached. The ICBM launcher is still up there too; it must be a mail van after all. Overall the train is much shorter without any Mongolian or Russian carriages, maybe ten coaches long. There is nothing to hang around for, so I wheel my bags down into the huge underpass and join the sea of people heading for the outside world.

All that separates me from a hot shower is finding a taxi willing to take a rough-looking farang with lots of bags to an address in the south-east of the city centre. After a few false starts, I find a one that is willing to take me for what sounds like a reasonable price, but I'm on guard to being scammed. My driver laughs a lot and says creepy things in English that concern me like, 'I have you now,' and, 'Where are we going?'

At the hotel, the concierge pretends that my bags are Louis Vuitton and whisks me up to a nice room on the 14th floor. As soon as he has left me alone I walk into the bathroom to play with the taps like they are a new invention or even witchcraft. Amazingly there is an unlimited amount of both hot and cold water. Even better, the air conditioning will serve up temperatures in the 20–25°C range. This is quite special, when for the last few days the only two available temperatures have been either +30°C or -25°C. I shall make the most of this thermal freedom.

Nine: Enter the Dragon

Day Thirteen, Beijing, China
Distance travelled so far: 11,112 km

All I need to do is press a button on the control panel beside my bed and the curtains to my room open themselves. My view from bed is of a grey smog-filled Christmas Day. I have to get up, though, to look down at street level. People looked well wrapped up and many wear face masks. I could spend all day in my lovely room, but I have things to do. I didn't spot it yesterday, but this time as I pass my desk I notice a neatly arranged cardboard courier envelope. Inside are my tickets to Hanoi and a nice letter from Sophie, my fixer here in Beijing. I have had too much else on to think about this, so I only have 30 seconds of mild panic before total relief, as I see that everything is in order. The feeling is rather like reading some good exam results that have arrived in the post.

My new little green ticket is highly unusual. Issued in China, but having to follow with international train ticket conventions, the languages on the ticket are Russian, German and Chinese. Nothing is in English. As I am to discover, very few Chinese ticket inspectors have ever seen one like it, as it is for a train that travels outside of China on a route few would think of undertaking. The ticket has been issued in two parts, from Beijing via Nanning to Pingxiang, and then from the Vietnamese border at Dong Dang to Hanoi. When I first looked at it I thought I would be actually going to Pyongyang, as it is handwritten in English. Another time perhaps. I text Sophie to tell her I have the packet, and then send a couple of emails to my fixers in the countries ahead. The next person I'm depending upon is Emily in Hanoi to sort out my Vietnamese sleeper reservations, and then Vi in Saigon to resolve my crossing of Cambodia, a country that is currently without a viable railway.

I have woken up this morning seriously smelling of sheep, to be more specific, spit-roast lamb. I feel like I must have ingested a whole one last night with my friend Alan (from carriage 6 on the Trans-Mong). He had heard of a place, buried deep in the *hutongs* (enclaves), that specialised in Chinese Muslim barbecue food, which was a meal that neither of us wanted to miss. The only problem was finding it. I met him outside a nearby subway stop in the early evening. Although we knew that we were close by there seemed to be no way of identifying on foot the hutong it was hidden in. I knew what to do. Rather like a special superpower, I waved down something I had discovered on a past visit, a strange sort of moped taxi resembling the Hong Kong Phooey mobile from the 1970s Hanna-Barbera cartoon. They can go anywhere and everywhere with seemingly no rules of the road or the pavement to follow. It is the quickest way anywhere as long as you are not involved in an accident, in which case you will probably die. Our short trip provides much entertainment and a few scares weaving through gaps in the traffic and backstreets, and delivers us right to the secret door of Tan Hua Lamb BBQ.

The driver smiles at me in a nice but vaguely menacing way and insists on double the agreed fare. Standing his ground, he tells me that his fare was per person. There are a few men sitting outside the restaurant smoking and observing our emerging disagreement. I can't work out if they are locals who hear this scam every day or if they are his friends. I'm normally a mild and relaxed person, but having travelled so far without being ripped off, I'm somehow enraged by this situation. I decide there and then that we are not going to pay him double, and pay him the fare we have agreed. Hoping he doesn't understand much English I tell Alan of my intentions, hoping he will be coming too. The driver isn't happy about this development, but we are off. I look behind after a few yards but spot no sword-wielding thugs chasing us. Hiding behind a wall we eventually double back and enter the restaurant when the coast is clear. I have just saved £2.50.

If getting to Tan Hua was dangerous, being inside it loaded up the risk factors considerably more. Not from hungry martial arts black belts, but from the lethal practice of a man who carries white-hot charcoal in buckets inches behind seated guests. If I were coming here again I would bring both a bucket of water and a first aid kit. After a short wait we get seated, and a man arrives with half a sheep and places it on a bar above the BBQ on our table. He offers some basic butchery advice in both Chinese and then sign language, before leaving us to it. Alan thinks he can handle this, and occasionally turns the animal on the spit as we drink local beer and watch how people are doing it on other tables around us. There is a delicious smell and lots of dripping fat by now, so we agree that it's ready. He picks up the scary knife and carves a few slices. The meat is utterly delicious, and we work our way through the joint in about an hour. When we think we have finished the chef comes around to inspect Alan's butchery skills and manages to carve even more meat from the carcass. After paying the ridiculously cheap bill we slip into the night, keeping an eye out for angry taxi drivers and their mates on the hutong rooftops. In fact, for the rest of my time in Beijing I keep turning around in case the Phooey mobile man has been following me seeking revenge for failing to pay him 20 yuan.

Putting all of this to the back of my mind, I make the most of my bathroom and find some clothes that don't smell of sheep before heading out to find some reasonable coffee. I spend the rest of the morning walking the grounds of the Summer Palace. It's cold but beautiful in the sunshine. Perhaps the most famous bridge in the city is here, the Jade Belt Bridge. Its steep arch looks like a recipe for disaster if you were to drive over it at any speed, but on foot it's pleasant enough to cross.

With my sightseeing done, the only other thing that I want to do today is to have a quick look inside Beijing West railway station. It's now the largest railway station in Asia, and I'm a bit confused by how and where my train will depart, as it will be my first experience of waiting rooms and gates that don't always correspond to departing platforms.

After my experiences on the Moscow metro, the subway in Beijing is easy to use. The station names might be alien, but at least they are written in English as well as Mandarin. When I arrive at Beijing West I realise the scale of the place by the fact that it is made up of two enormous concourses and I'm in the wrong one. The main problem with my idea of a recce is that you can't get into the station concourse without a valid ticket. When I reach the front of the queue outside the entrance the guard inspects my little green ticket and looks unsure. He summons his supervisor, who also doesn't recognise my ticket, so he calls his manager. I'm blessed, as he is a younger man and speaks a little English. He thinks my request to come into his station a day before I'm due to depart is a little bit weird, but he decides I'm not a threat. He makes me promise not to go down onto the platform before waving at the guards on the x-ray machine to let me pass.

There is nothing overly unusual about this place other than its scale. It is a station on steroids, big enough to manage the volume of passengers. Escalators rise past an electronic departures board towards the waiting rooms. I'm confused because with my soft class ticket

I might be able to use a VIP lounge, but am not sure how I will then be able to depart to my platform, which seems to use a different lounge. The key is understanding that all the waiting rooms and some lounges open out onto a bridge that crosses the platforms. You can be in waiting room 6 for your train, but it will leave from platform 9. Confused? I was. I managed to speak to a guard who helpfully shows me where I will need to go. It seems I'm not a VIP here, and the soft class lounge is not much better than the correct waiting room for my train. That's all I need to know, and satisfied I know where I'll be going, I get back on the subway to Guomao on the Batong line, near to where I'm staying.

Guomao station is near to the entrance to the China World Mall, a huge shopping centre, and I decide some retail therapy might be good for me before getting back on the rails. If nothing else I can walk back to my hotel through its warm interior rather than in the frosty smog outside. Up escalators, down escalators, round endless curved walkways, I head slowly back to base. The trouble is I have lost my bearings and seem to keep reappearing at a famous international handbag store next to a Seattle-based coffee shop. I try again and my navigation ends with the same result. The first man I ask for directions is really helpful. So helpful in fact that he doesn't want me to go anywhere without escorting me somewhere else. The trouble is he's a scammer, albeit a nice scammer, selling tickets to a one-off never-to-be-repeated art sale from his grandfather who runs a prestigious art school. This is well-known scam in the book of Chinese scams, so I have to say goodbye to him and find another way out. Just when I think I have broken the gravity of the handbag store, I pass a familiar-looking designer store, and lo and behold there it is in front of me, I'm back there again. In the end I find a security man who points and makes a lot of left and right gestures combined with up and down gestures like he might be teaching me how to swim. Vitally I learn that I can escape via the next-door world trade centre, and this gives me something I can ask directions for. If you don't read Mandarin signs you could spend all weekend in this place trying.

I'm delighted to finally make it back at my hotel. It's time to make the most of its facilities before getting on the train to Hanoi. It has quite a good nightclub downstairs, and I spend the evening with the cigar-smoking expats at the bar discussing Shanghai property prices. It's a very different world to the one I'm living in.

Ten: The Restaurant at the End of the T5

Day Sixteen, Beijing, China
Distance travelled so far: 11,112 km

Beijing time (GMT +8)

Station	Arrival	Departure
Beijing West		16:08
Shijiazhuang	19:00	19:03
Zhengzhou	22:50	22:56

My train today from Beijing West has no glamorous name: it's known simply as the T5 until we reach Dong Dang on the Vietnamese border, when it will become the M2. In China, the high-speed train numbers all begin with the letter a G, the fast trains with a D, and the (slower) express trains with a T. These make limited stops at large stations only. The only slower long-distance trains begin with the letter K. These are the same type of train, just making more stops.

I can't manage my luggage on the subway, so spend an hour crawling in a proper taxi through the traffic to the station. Thanks to my reconnaissance visit I find the right entrance without fuss and process my bags through the security check. It's all going quite well until I somehow manage to fall onto the x-ray belt, nearly heading into the machine after my bags. So much for looking like a seasoned rail adventurer.

I am prepared for how to find my waiting room and where the train will depart from – but not for the number of people who have the same plan. In waiting room 8 there are thousands of us milling around ready for the off. I eventually manage to persuade a sceptical woman inspector that I could be suitable material for the adjacent soft class lounge. My ticket is for a seat in a second class soft four-berth cabin. There is no first class on this train.

From an almost comfortable seat in the roped-off area I have a good view of the chaos around me. The passengers shout a lot and carry amazing quantities of luggage, mostly wrapped in cardboard or plastic bags. For once I don't feel quite so guilty about my big bag. Officials wander around shouting things at the crowd, but these are mainly unheard over the din of all that is going on. At one end of the waiting room are the gates, each with a display of the next train to board, shown as the train number and the final destination.

You can't get onto the platform of a modern Chinese station until the train is called. Each waiting room has several gates but the trains are called at just one of them. I'm well back in the queue for our gate and use my luggage to stop everyone from just barging past.

Queuing etiquette is still in its infancy in this land. When it's my turn at the gate the guard does not recognise my international ticket, but lets me go anyway for fear of a stampede behind me. I struggle down the stairs to the platform to find a seriously long train, more than 20 carriages. I'm in search of carriage L2. The conductress won't let me on carriage 2. She points further back down the train and I keep walking. I discover that if you keep going up the numbered carriages past carriage 11, you eventually reach L1 and L2; these are the soft class international sleeper carriages.

Once allowed onto the sleeper I'm shown to an empty compartment right by the guard's cabin at the near end. It's a four-berth, and my first impression is that it is really comfy. There is much chintz to the décor and complimentary rubber slippers and chopsticks are provided; surely an auspicious sign. My first impression of the guards is that they seem helpful and professional. I suspect they are used to dealing with Westerners, but it is interesting that I have not spotted a single foreigner in the whole of Beijing West railway station, nor any on this train. Where are they hiding?

Several passengers look into my compartment and decide to join me, but the guards move them on. At first I think they might be isolating me in case I'm carrying a Western disease, but I decide that the reason has something to do with being an international passenger and being separated for Customs reasons.

Once we set off I wait in the compartment to see if anyone is coming to join me. I don't want to leave the place for fear of it being taken over by other passengers looking to spread out from fuller compartments. I wait for the conductor to come and collect my ticket. He seems to know all about my ticket and my journey, which is most encouraging after my experience at the station. My ticket is taken away and I'm given a little gold plastic card with a number in its place. Free now to move around I head towards the restaurant carriage, which is only three coaches away. Some passengers are perhaps ten or more carriages away from here. That's a serious walk and perhaps 40 doors to deal with.

As I have discovered, the drill in a Chinese train restaurant is that you look at the menu, choose what you want and pay before sitting down. You pay the person dressed like a policeman. But the menu is in Mandarin and as I have no idea what anything is, I just ignore this and go and sit down, playing my farang credentials. The other passengers stare at me, but I ignore them and just play cool like I eat noodles in places like this all the time. My Chinese restaurant party trick is the reverse menu look-up. All I need to do is to point at dishes other people are eating then get them to show me which dish that is on the menu. When the waiter comes I can just point at a line on my menu and he might even think I can read it. I order some beef and fried rice and a bottle of cloned Chinese Budweiser. That's not my choice, but it's the only beer they have. It comes warm, fresh out of a cardboard box at the end of the corridor. Never mind. As I make the most of my warm Bud, the policeman comes over to briefly question me. Actually, with just one word: 'Beef?' Maybe he gets to decide if the person ordering it is suitable to have such a dish.

Back in my compartment, I have realised that I have no idea where and when this train is going to stop: I have idiotically forgotten to print off a timetable of my own. There is a timetable at the end of my carriage in the form of a mathematical Mandarin table of equations, but I'm more likely to decipher the Enigma code than work out where we are going by using it. I vaguely remember that I'm going to have to get off the train for some purpose in Nanning tomorrow evening, but until then it's going to be a magical mystery tour. At least I know I'm staying on until then.

Day Eighteen, Changsha, China
Distance travelled so far: 12,589 km

Beijing time (GMT +8)

Station	Arrival	Departure
Changsha	07:31	07:43
Hengyang	09:31	09:39
Yongzhou	11:39	11:49
Guilin	14:50	14:58
Liuzhou	17:02	17:08
Nanning	20:10	21:15

Last night, I didn't do much other than read and sleep. I feel a bit like a soldier heading towards the front line and taking advantage of any spare time to rest and prepare. I shall be in action most of tonight, so it's a day of train-based rest and recuperation.

In the night I woke a couple of times and sauntered down to the toilets at the far end. In this carriage, there is a big communal washroom and then next door two toilets, one Western, one squatter. Both really stink of stale cigarettes. The official policy is no smoking on this train, but it's not like an aircraft – there are no smoke alarms in the bathrooms. I can't resist peeking out the window from time to time. At one point in the night I drew back my curtains to see we were at a station named after the 1980s rap music sensation, the Wuchang (Clan).

Once I have made up my bed I fix myself a cup of coffee and settle down for a read. I'm quite quickly getting used to the way this train works, and I really like it. If you want to catch a slice of China on the move, then just leave the door to your compartment open. Not only do the locals come to stare, but you get to meet all the people selling things door to door. These range from food and beverages, magazines, and sets of nail clippers through to things like iPads that have probably not been designed in California. It's like a Chinese home shopping channel on the rails.

Having recently read *The Boys from Brazil*, I was also surprised to see no less than seven identical female train guards walk past. Are they sisters, or do all Chinese women look the same in uniform? They must be the product of a strict railway finishing school.

The pace of my day is dead slow. In fact it's the first day on this journey where I have elected to do very little. Getting off at the stops isn't much fun on this train, as the platforms become packed with people and there is a risk of being swept away in the crowd. With no timetable I just watch the sun pass overhead and down the east side of the train. The scenery is a mixture of flat agricultural landscape peppered with sprawling concrete factories and power plants for much of the day, but as we progress southwards I can see giant karst hills in the direction of Guilin. The view is rather spoiled by the chimneys, but the pollution makes for a colourful sunset later on. My view is accompanied by the slightly obscure but brilliant 'Hocus Pocus' by Dutch band Focus.

With time to enjoy a leisurely dinner in the restaurant carriage before the fun begins, I experience one of those comedy moments when everybody stops eating and drops their chopsticks to stare at me until they discover the purpose of my visit to the restaurant. The crew shout things to each other in Mandarin. I can only guess at their meaning: 'We've got another one of those white farang types here. He's sitting down. Who is going to have to deal with him?' It all works out fine though. My revised restaurant party trick is that I have now memorised the menu dishes by their price, so I can point to them and act like I can read the menu.

My meal tonight consists of what was probably a breakfast menu dish (oops!), scrambled eggs and ham, followed by a rather good spicy beef and cabbage soup, freshly cooked by a team of two chefs. My only disappointment was the lack of Great Wall wine on board, a China Railway personal favourite. Tired of warm beer I try a shot of the local spirit instead, and wish that I hadn't as it tastes of paraffin mixed with old socks.

The T5 seems to be cracking on, having made only three or four stops in the last 15 hours. It's far smoother than the Trans-Mong, with much better potential to sleep. I only wish it went all the way to Hanoi, but it reconfigures at Nanning, then only goes as far as the frontier at Dong Dang. No one on board understands me when I say that I'm going to Hanoi but they all know a city in the same place on the map called Hennei.

As we pull into Nanning a sea of people leave the train, a tide sweeping them down the platform and over the walkways. I'm told I can leave my bag in my compartment, but for some reason I have to get off the train and stay in an international waiting room. Escorted personally by a conductress I feel a bit like a schoolboy taking a plane trip alone. The lady says she is going to come and collect me and escort me back to the train when the time comes. I have no idea when that is likely to be. The practical reason for all this is apparently a lot of shunting and reconfiguring of the T5 to prepare it for the run to the border. They obviously don't know that I'm a veteran of cataclysmically big shunts in the bogie sheds of Terespol and Erlian.

The international lounge in Nanning is full of slightly dodgy-looking middle-aged men in black leather jackets smoking and fiddling with their Blackberry-type devices. A Chinese version of 'Blind Date' blares from a television across the room and a security lady waves a metal detector wand in the general direction of anyone coming in. The girls on 'Blind Date' are easy on the eye, and everybody seems mesmerised by what's on the screen.

Time passes slowly and I feel uncomfortable to be separated from my luggage and to have no idea when I need to be ready to leave. After a couple of hours of Chinese television I'm ready to slit my wrists, so I'm very pleased to see my escort arrive to take me back to the train. We return to platform 13, but it's deserted now. I hadn't realised, but I'm more valuable cargo than I had first thought; she has had to physically sign me out of the lounge and back over to the train guard. I have my own black A4 file. I hope it only says nice things about me.

My big surprise when I see the T5 again is what's left of it. There are now just two carriages sitting at the platform. I thought that the other people in the lounge were coming with us, but apparently not. There must be another international service heading into central Asia. I ask my escort about other passengers before she leaves and she says no one else is coming. The T5 is now my private train consisting of me, my carriage, a spare carriage and a luggage van plus about ten guards. The conductor also confirms it is a non-stop train specifically to convey me to the Vietnamese side of the Chinese border at Pingxiang. I can't wait to see how this frontier crossing goes.

As the train is much smaller now, I am able to take a gratuitous engine shot as the new locomotive arrives to couple up with us. I'm mildly rebuked for doing this, but I figure that the whole benefit of a private train is that it goes when you want it to. I couldn't take any photographs of it earlier today, as a 20-carriage walk and no timetable would have made such an endeavour a bit high risk.

We gently pull out of Nanning at 22:56 with about three hours to run to the Chinese side of the frontier. The guards settle in for a rest as they have no one other than me to worry about. Sitting back in my berth I'm wondering if this development has any downside. I hope the Vietnamese authorities don't single me out for any special treatment as the only migrant tonight.

The driver toots his horn every minute or so, which isn't easy to sleep through, but I can't fault his excitement to get me to the border on time. It is possible that he was hooting like this all last night as well, but you don't hear it at the back of a much longer train. In front of my bathroom there is now a sign in Mandarin hanging by a chain. I assume it says something like 'Opening this door may result in death'. I do my best to rest, but don't want to chance mission failure by missing my connection in Dong Dang. But the adrenaline of crossing an unknown border alone in the jungle and at night keeps me going.

Eleven: Rumble in the Jungle

Day Nineteen, Pingxiang, China
Distance travelled so far: 13,668 km

Beijing time (GMT +8)

Station	Arrival	Departure
Pingxiang	01:05	02:40

Hanoi time (GMT+7)

Dong Dang	02:21	03:50
Hanoi	08:10	

I listen to the sound of silence apart from the humming of the of the locomotive's diesel engine as we wait for clearance at the Chinese frontier station of Pingxiang. A very polite young Chinese official has checked my visa and left with my passport, which he even tells me he is going to stamp. The crew are mainly in bed, so it's like the Mary Celeste on the train. No one is telling me what to do, so I'm just sitting in my compartment – or should I say my train – waiting for new orders.

At about 02:30 Beijing time we leave Pingxiang and creep through a small jungle with our lights turned off. Emerging back into the open on a single track, we pull into Dong Dang, on the Vietnamese side of the border. What now?

One of the guards comes to get me and tells me to follow him with my luggage. Climbing down from the carriage I find it unexpectedly cold outside and I shiver a little as we wait for a posse of Chinese guards to form up by the train. Everything is dark around the train, but the station has multi-coloured lights around the trees and looks more like a deserted beach bar than a railway station. As we cross the tracks an immigration man steps out of the shadows and introduces himself. It feels more like a Cold War prisoner exchange than a rail connection. The Vietnamese official inspects the small pile of passports belonging to each of the guards on the T5. He doesn't stamp them and lets the guard party return to their train. Rather nicely they say goodbye to me and wish me well. 'Bye Bye' seems to be a universally understood word. I'm on my own now.

Following the man up the steps to the station, I arrive in an empty waiting room. He asks me to take a seat whilst he takes my passport away. As the lights flicker on I can see that the room is vintage and wooden. There are framed posters on the walls promoting possible Vietnamese tourist destinations, and at one end of the room is a folding screen that I suspect hides a medical inspection area. I had read that Vietnam conducts a full medical on cross-border travellers arriving from China by land. But tonight I can't see anyone dressed in a white coat, and there is no nurse with a pair of rubber gloves and a thermometer.

I don't have too long to worry about my medical as the man returns with my passport, and everything is apparently in order. There are no declarations, no Customs inspections, no health check, and in fact no paperwork at all to complete. Unsure what my next move might be, he then very kindly shows me to two deserted red and blue Vietnamese carriages standing at the opposite platform. I know from my ticket that these will become the continuation of the T5, now in Vietnam known as the M2. There is no sign of life inside the M2, but the immigration man unlocks it and opens up one of the doors like he has had to do this before. Inside I think that I can hear snoring. I thank the official as he helps me lift my luggage up onto the carriage and we say goodbye. That has to be one of the weirdest rail border crossings ever.

I try not to make too much noise as I get my bags down the corridor for fear of waking the sleeping occupants. I don't have a compartment number, so I just choose one in the middle of the carriage and move in. The style here is rustic, with rough-cut wooden panels and red curtains. There are four bunk beds, each with a blanket and a pillow. It's slightly damp and in need of a good clean. Selecting one of the lower berths, I sit down and try to relax in my new surroundings. As I take off my boots a mouse appears from under my bed and scuttles between my feet before heading out into the corridor.

There is no point unpacking; I just need to make myself comfortable for the next few hours. I can hear activity outside, and a small shunter engine is coupled to the front of the two carriages. A couple of toots of the horn and we are off down the native gauge line, which is the same as the Russian rail gauge up to the Mongolian border. Despite the Vietnamese gauge being wider than the Chinese one, the ancient carriage rocks and sways like a boat on a rough sea.

It is perhaps ironic that after my couple of weeks' training in jungle temperatures on Chinese trains, my first night in the jungles of Southeast Asia is spent in an unheated, damp and freezing cold Vietnamese carriage. I spend what's left of the night in my compartment with the mouse, who I have named Basil. It's bearable, but only in the same way that a bivouac at Camp Two on Everest is bearable; it's not a place you want to spend a lot of time in. I have never been keener for the sun to rise and warm the inside of the train before. I'm not afraid of mice, but it does cross my mind that Basil might invite his friends to our compartment and make a nest in my bed while I sleep. So I move up to a top bunk, not that it would make much difference.

The other issue is that I have some itchy bites on my legs, and as they are in neat rows I think these are the tell-tale signs of bedbugs. I'm going to chuck everything in the hotel laundry when I reach Hanoi. It is so cold this morning that I have to get my down jacket out; I hope it is free of any critters as it's very hard to clean. On the upside, I haven't seen any mosquitoes in here. In these parts they are quite malaria drug-resistant, which reminds me to get some pills out of my first aid box.

The train crosses a lot of bridges as it passes through the outskirts of the city. A scruffy man pokes his head in and asks me for my ticket. It seems a bit late in the journey, but I show him my international ticket anyway. He notes its number and hands it back saying 'Hanoi' to me. That's good; we are on the same page. Pleased to be escaping from the M2, I say farewell to Basil at the Ga Ha Noi. He must be used to the cold.

I notice that there are several men dangling off the footplate of the little shunter that has been pulling us from Dong Dang. This must be the wild west of Vietnam. They shout and wave at me. It turns out that I am walking in the wrong direction, but I don't like to admit it. Instead I do as the locals do, and cut across the tracks. It's not easy with a big bag on wheels, and I have to lift it over each rail. As soon as I have done it I'm cross with myself as I have just taken an unnecessary risk. I glance back at the M2 before leaving the main platform and rather hope I don't have to use that train again, at least until they invest in some better carriages.

Twelve: SAM City

Day Twenty, Hanoi, Vietnam
Distance travelled so far: 13,841 km

The streets of Hanoi are still foggy but busy at this time of the morning. I'm resigned to the inevitability of paying a crazily inflated price for a taxi, and I'm ready with a pile of low denomination dong banknotes. It's an expensive trip but I'm in no mood to spend an hour finding a cheaper fare. When I reach the reception of my hotel the news isn't what I wanted to hear. My room won't be ready for six hours, so I decide to set up camp in the bar. This is partly a tactical decision, as I feel that having a smelly Englishman with potentially bedbug-infested luggage strewn around the sophisticated environment of the French bar might focus the minds of the management on finding me a room.

Hot coffee, little biscuits and tasteful music soothe my nerves. The women behind the bar wear their national costume, the Ao Dai, and greet customers in French. I spread my gear out near a man playing a

159

piano and get on the internet for the first time in a week. My mail account has been blocked in China, so now I can catch up on news from the other side of the world. I'm just finishing my second cup of frothy coffee when as if by magic the immaculately dressed duty manager appears and tells me that sadly, my room isn't ready yet, but they do have a nicer room on a higher floor that might suit my needs and at no extra cost of course. Would I be interested? Before he can even finish his sentence, I'm packing up and we are soon headed for the lift. Keep up at the back, Mr Duty Manager!

Once installed in my room I bundle all the clothes that I have been wearing into a single laundry bag, then seal it in a plastic bag before decontaminating myself in the shower. I consider writing something like 'Danger – bedbugs' on the laundry form, but decide against it as this isn't an outbreak of ebola or Nile fever. Once it has been collected I head out of the hotel for some supplies, most vitally a replacement cable for my camera, which has just failed in southern China. In my experience cables always fail, unless you are carrying a spare cable. Then they never fail.

The rest of my day is spent cruising the chaotic streets of the old quarter of Hanoi. One of the enduring good things the French did in Vietnam – other than import its skills in baking, brewing and the guillotine – was to popularise coffee and cafe culture. Coffee in Vietnam has become quite specialised to local tastes. Cold coffee, often with condensed milk, is more popular than hot coffee, but even this is an art form with a special little cup-sized metal dripper called a phin. Today Vietnam grows and exports over 20 per cent of the world's coffee. Much of this is the less fashionable Robusta bean, but they also grow Arabica beans in the highlands. I'm actually a fan of both, as you get a bigger caffeine hit off the cheaper beans.

I find a promising-looking coffee roaster down a little side street and check all the blends he has on offer. Each bean crop has several levels of quality, usually ranging from A to AAA, and on top of this is the organic certification. But the one that catches my eye is described as 'weasel'. After a careful conversation, it transpires that in the same way as the Indonesians produce Kopi Luwak, a rather expensive bean that has been excreted by a civet cat, the ever-enterprising Vietnamese are experimenting with weasels. The weasel eats the beans, digests them and excretes them, still whole, which gives them a unique flavour.

I settle on some double-roasted AAA weasel coffee, but there is a further decision. Do I want the top grade organic version? I consider this carefully. Is it the weasel that is organic, or the beans? The roaster understands what I'm asking, and it turns out that you can't certify the weasel as it lives freely in the forest, only the beans. Grade 1 weasel coffee costs about $65 a kilo, considerably cheaper than its famous Indonesian rival. I decide to buy a couple of bags to take home and serve to the few people who doubted my resolve to complete this journey.

Day Twenty-One, Hanoi, Vietnam
Distance travelled so far: 13,841 km

Hanoi time (GMT +7)

Station	Arrival	Departure
Hanoi		19:30
Phu Ly	20:34	20:37
Nam Dinh	21:11	21:14
Nam Binh	21:46	21:49
Thanh Hoa	22:55	22:58

My first call of the day was to visit what most travellers call B-52 Lake, situated in the north of the city, but its real name is Huu Tiep Lake. Here the remains of a bomber shot down in 1972 still poke out of the water, but a small crumpled pile of grey metal is all that you can see these days. When I first visited Vietnam in the 1992, the city was full of war junk. Kids' playgrounds across the country were mainly made up of abandoned tanks, anti-aircraft guns and missile launchers. The scrap metal merchants have since had their day, but there are still a few interesting sites around the city. Hanoi didn't feature in many Hollywood war movies, with one notable exception. *Flight of the Intruder* was released in 1991. It wasn't a box office smash, but remains an interesting if slightly far-fetched story. It culminates with an attack run in an A6-B Intruder aircraft to destroy a fictitious park full of surface-to-air missiles in Hanoi, which was called SAM City.

With my bags packed, my laundry deloused and my bag full of interesting provisions, I set out on my last day in the city to sample some local dishes. My lunch lasts several hours thanks to a local chap who calls himself Johnny. He knows exactly where to take me. The idea is to try just one dish at each place we visit – the dish the place is famous for. Johnny tells me that everything is possible, which I take to be coded language for eating things off the menu in some places. Call me unadventurous, but I ask him to keep me away from any dog- and insect-based dishes.

Our first meal of the day is all about duck, accompanied by salad, shallots and some aniseed-tasting local herb. The secret is in the dipping sauce. Next up is a street snack of rice with pork sausage stuffed with paté of undisclosed origin. We then move onto a meal of sea worm fritters. The worms look disgusting, but once in fritter form they taste surprisingly good. Next are some rather good mushroom and shrimp dumpling rolls with coriander fried onions. Finally, there is fish. It is apparently unusual to get fish on the street, so we go inside a proper restaurant for this. We feast on catfish, fried and then served with rice paper rolls, noodles, peanuts, herbs and cucumber.

With a week's worth of food consumed, we finish at a place to drink the local draft home brew beer, Bia-Hoi. Bia-Hoi is colonial French technology. A bar simply brews a new barrel of it each week, then serves it into glasses straight out of a tap, over ice. Cheap and delicious. But sadly there is no time to get too comfortable here as I have a train to catch.

Of course, there is no single train called The Reunification Express in Vietnam. That would be like Virgin East Coast calling the 08:30 train from Kings Cross to Edinburgh the Flying Scotsman. Having said that I have a ticket on the SE1, so I'm going to imagine it is the closest thing to this mythical train, going all the way from Hanoi to Saigon in three days. My destination is Da Nang in central Vietnam, around 15 hours south of Hanoi, depending on the weather and the number of water buffalo on the line.

After my experiences in China, getting on board this train proves to be incredibly straightforward. There are no big queues inside the station, passengers are well behaved and the platform is opened an hour before departure, with just a cursory ticket check. The train that pulls in on the southbound line is about ten carriages long, consisting of soft and hard sleepers, soft seat carriages and a restaurant. Even though this is one of the country's most prestigious trains, it is immediately clear that it has seen better days.

My carriage is towards the back of the train, and I find myself in a four-berth second-class soft compartment, sharing with a chap called Rob from London, travelling to Hue, and Mr Chi, a Vietnamese Canadian, travelling with his sister's daughter, Ram. They are on their way home to Can Tho, right down in the Mekong delta. The SE1 is definitely more comfortable that the M2 from Dong Dang. It's pretty grubby, but not so bad as to be a problem. The temperature inside is set for human habitation, and has no obvious signs of rodent or insect infestation.

The atmosphere on board is quite lively. Music blares from the corridor and people shout at each other from opposite ends of the carriage. The conductor makes occasional chatty announcements on a PA, but I have no idea what he is saying. At one end of the carriage there are flushing toilets and an open plan wash room. The doors between the carriages flap and bang with the sway of the train and provide some ventilation.

The staff are quite informal by Chinese standards, and perch on collapsible chairs at the end of each carriage drinking from proper tea sets whilst sending text messages to their friends. They don't seem to have their own compartment. There is also a strange arrangement in our carriage with a woman who appears to live in a cupboard. The problem is that she can't lie down with the door closed, so her feet stick out and the opening is covered with a purpose-made curtain. I have no idea if she is on board in an official capacity.

Rob is up for a beer, so we walk forwards nine coaches to the restaurant carriage. There is not much food on offer, but we find all the off-duty staff here smoking and drinking. We sit down next to a couple of locals who quickly move on in case they catch something from us. Icy cans of 333 Export cost 15,000 dong or 43 pence each. I love ordering this beer, as it allows me to practise one of my few passable Vietnamese words. 'Three' is pronounced *ba*, so a 333 beer is simply *ba ba ba* – a very satisfying piece of schoolboy Vietnamese. Over a couple of cold ones Rob tells me he is planning to travel from Hue down to Hoi An by scooter. I think he might be mad, but who am I to judge?

Life in the soft seat carriages we pass though on the way back looks tough. It's packed, and quite a few people sit in the aisle on little plastic stools that they have brought with them. People are either watching a Vietnamese soap on the television screen above the door, or slumped over, covered by their coats and trying to sleep. I do my best not to bump into them, by anticipating the rolling motion of the carriage.

Preparing for bed in my lower bunk, I decide I need some help getting some rest and decide that it's safe enough to take a sleeping pill. This is based on a risk assessment of my fellow passengers combined with the time I'm going to need to get off the train the next day. With the drug administered I lie back and wait to start feeling sleepy. All I can feel to begin with is indigestion, as I have eaten too much duck and too many worms today. Also I can't stop thinking about bedbugs now. The bedding looks clean as the train today has started in Hanoi. The bedding isn't changed when passengers get off, just carefully refolded, so it's second-hand to passengers down the line. I have a sheet sleeping bag with me, and I really must start to use it.

Eventually I fall asleep, but wake every time we approach a station as a pre-recorded tape is played selling the business and cultural highlights of each city before we arrive in it. I don't know what they were thinking – might passengers just suddenly decide to change their plans and get off, from what they heard? Then after the marketing pitch the conductor says his words. Just in case you aren't fully awake by this point, an attendant enters the compartment collecting and refolding sheets for empty beds.

Day Twenty-Two, Hue, Vietnam
Distance travelled so far: 14,201 km

Hanoi time (GMT +7)

Station	Arrival	Departure
Cho Sy	00:51	00:54
Vinh	01:34	01:41
Yen Trung	02:04	02:07
Huong Pho	02:59	03:02
Dong Ha	07:33	07:36
Hue	08:48	08:56
Da Nang	11:26	11:41

Rubbing my eyes and getting accustomed to daylight I sit up and find I'm the last up. Rob has got off at Hue, so we have now had a spare berth to put our bags on until someone else claims it. Mr Chi smiles and offers me some odd-looking fruit. 'Lunch,' he declares, but it is only half past ten. I need coffee before lunch, but I discover that the samovars are unserviceable throughout the train. Ram sips an iced coffee from the catering trolley that passes our compartment every now and then. I wonder if I dare risk Vietnamese Railway ice as well, but I decide not, and instead choose to breakfast on Coke and fried rice. Mr Chi tucks in to some fried chicken saying it's very good, but I have my doubts. He tells me his story over our catering trolley feast. He had to leave Vietnam in 1979 and migrated to Hong Kong, and then to Canada. He was one of the Chinese-descended families that left when they were persecuted by the government after the war. At that time these refugees were known as the Vietnamese boat people. Now a relatively wealthy Canadian citizen, he is now returning to Vietnam for the second time to see his family, and also escorting his niece home.

This morning I am able to enjoy what must be one of the most picturesque railway scenes in Asia, the Hai Van pass. As we cross the mountains from the central highlands, I can see a long bar of sand extending outwards to a river mouth where it meets the sea. It is stunningly beautiful and at the same time reminds me of Charlie's Point from Francis Ford Coppola's epic 1979 war movie, *Apocalypse Now*. My choice of music is perhaps predictably from this period too; Martha and the Vandellas, the Beach Boys and the Rolling Stones make up today's soundtrack.

Checking the timetable, we seem to be running about two hours late. There is just a single track in places, so we have to wait for the northbound trains to pass us in stations along the way, which is slowing us down. But I'm in no hurry today, and feel very relaxed if a little sleep-deprived.

Da Nang station remains relatively small and uncomplicated. In 1972 the city had the busiest single runway in the world and was the most northerly airfield in the Republic of South Vietnam, being only 60 km south of the Demilitarised Zone or DMZ, the dividing line between the north and the south. Today despite its small station, the city is the fourth biggest in the country and a hotel building boom has transformed its outlying coastline. All that is needed are tourists to fill the rooms.

Although I'm nearly three hours late, a man from my hotel is still there waiting outside to meet me. He hands me a cold towel and proceeds to squeeze my luggage into his small car. Between the station and the beach is perhaps one of the most exciting bridges in Southeast Asia today. The Dragon Bridge was opened in 2013 at a cost of over 1.5 trillion dong, and every weekend at 9pm it breathes fire and water in a spectacular show for the residents of the city.

Just half an hour after getting off the SE1, I'm in my shorts and walking on the China Beach, my feet being gently washed by the Pacific Ocean. This is the very same beach that American serviceman used to let off steam whilst on R&R all those years ago. Today is New Year's Eve in the Western calendar, but I'm far too tired to celebrate it. As I sit on my balcony in a colonial wicker chair watching tourists play volleyball and the moody sun setting over the ocean, without warning a big bat dives at me. Then another. I'm under attack. Unclear on the rabies position, I decide to retreat inside my room where I can still hear the waves from my bed. Living on trains makes you really appreciate the nicer things in life. A rail adventurer has to take the rough with the smooth, and this is bliss.

After a slow start New Year's Day gives me a chance to further explore China Beach. On the highway outside my hotel is a place that will fix anything. In one transaction you can get your laundry done, have a massage, buy a bottle of Mekong whisky and book a tour to the nearby Marble Mountains.

I could stay in this place for several weeks, but feel the need to keep moving. But before I get back on the rails I have arranged to stay in the nearby ancient port town of Hoi An for a few days. There is no railway station there, so it's a short journey by bus.

Thirteen: Pho Metal Jacket

Day Twenty-Three, Hoi An, Vietnam
Distance travelled so far: 14,613 km

Stanley Kubrick shot much of his 1987 war film *Full Metal Jacket* in London's docklands, with imported palm trees planted in rubbish skips. I don't think any films from the American war have actually been filmed in Vietnam – but if Kubrick's art director had given him storyboards for inspiration, they would all have shown places near where I am now staying in central Vietnam.

I have taken a bus about 30 km south of Da Nang to Cau Dai beach, where I'm staying on the outskirts of the 16th-century fishing village, Hoi An. It has been declared a UNESCO world heritage site, but long before this cars were banned, and nothing new has been built in the old town for a lifetime. Life is good here. It's very a beautiful place, and pretty cheap.

The town caters to travellers and backpackers. It is the sort of place that you can get anything done in, so I have spent the afternoon moving between the optician, tailor, hairdresser and pharmacy. To do this

I need to frequently cross the 18th-century Japanese bridge, very much the centrepiece of tourism for the town. My problem here is not the crowds, but that there is a man trying to charge foreigners to cross. Weaving and ducking, I avoid him for my first couple of crossings, but he catches me eventually and has something to say in lively Vietnamese about my antics. Out of principle I refuse to buy a ticket and walk downriver to a less touristy bridge. Next time I will have to merge better into a tour group.

The locals know exactly what the tourists want to buy. Down the street from my hairdresser I find a fake DVD shop that has a top shelf filled with every single American war film, and even the Vietnam Top Gear Special. There seems to be a set of ten carefully selected movies for tourists in most places, and this is made up of: *Apocalypse Now* (1979), *Platoon* (1986), *We Were Soldiers* (2002), *Full Metal Jacket* (1987), *Good Morning Vietnam* (1987), *Hamburger Hill* (1987), *Casualties of War* (1989), *The Deer Hunter* (1978), *The Quiet American* (2002) and *Indochine* (1992).

Strangely *Air America* is nowhere to be seen. I guess the Vietnamese feel it was made before Robert Downey Jr was at his best. I would like to see more cult stuff on offer, though, maybe the much underrated *Uncommon Valour* (1983) starring Gene Hackman, Fred Ward and a very young Patrick Swayze. I also think that *Flight of the Intruder* (1991) should be in wider circulation.

Last night I couldn't stop myself from watching *Apocalypse Now* before turning in. I feel strangely almost on set, but now 35 years after it was filmed. I have almost perfected my Robert Duvall 'Colonel Killgore' impersonation, all the way from 'I love the smell of napalm in the morning' through to 'someday this war is going to be over'.

My alarm sounds early the following morning. I have arranged to go on a deep dive into the local cuisine, arguably the best in Vietnam. My tutors are a retired Australian couple, Neville and Colleen, who meet me for coffee at 06:30 at the alarmingly named Tiger Market. Neville introduces me to a man known as Jimmy, who walks with me around the place like a proud Vietnamese uncle. Dressed in a distinctive black pork pie hat and matching leather waistcoat, Jimmy is an ARVN (the army of Southern Vietnam) veteran who has to get around on just one leg, the other having been lost to a landmine in 1970. Together we enjoy some *Pho Bo*, the famous breakfast dish of beef and noodles. It is self-assembly, and I add my own lime juice, chilli sauce, fish sauce and soy sauce. The noodle master wears a t-shirt inscribed with words Pho Metal Jacket.

We leave the market without seeing any tigers and head down a papaya tree-lined road to find Madam Khanh. She is famous in Hoi An for her *Banh Mi*, an amazing French bread sandwich. Some even call her the Bahn Mi Queen. Today she is on top form and even poses for a photograph with me whilst she carefully combines the contents of my sandwich.

The rest of the morning is a bit of a blur of gourmet street food, but I do remember the *Bahn Xeo*, a savoury crepe with pork, shrimp & bean sprouts, the *Cao Lau* noodles, whose flavour comes from the local well water; and *Thit Nuong*, street meat marinated in lemongrass, turmeric and honey.

I'm really touched to find out that Neville uses his guiding to raise money for local Agent Orange victims in his own quiet way. You can't not want to help. After saying goodbye and feeling I may never need to eat again, I lie on the beach and watch the surf crash on the hot sand.

I have one more spare day before I am due back on the rails, and I have decided to make the most of it. My plan is a spot of motorcycling, but not of the conventional kind. In 1940 Stalin had instructed his generals to make a motorbike that could provide mobility to his special forces. Their resulting invention was the Ural motorbike with its powerful and dependable 500cc engine. Part of the solution was not just the bike itself, but also a cleverly designed sidecar.

My driver is a well-dressed and quietly spoken man called Guan. He introduces me to our bike, gifted by the Soviet Union to North Vietnam, where it served as police transport for much of its life. It used to have a crew of three, and space for a detainee. Still in its police colours of red and white, it also retains its flashing lights and a working siren, but I'm instructed not to use this much as it scares the water buffalo.

Guan gives the kick starter a couple of big boots and the reluctant engine roars into life. Settling into the sidecar I have a great view all round. What a great way to travel. We set off on Highway 1, the road that connects the length of Vietnam along the coast. Rumbling along with a satisfying sound and smelling of burning oil I can't help but grin and wave at anyone who stares at us. Although we are wearing open-face helmets it is still quite easy to have a chat as we drive along. To me this is cooler than *Easy Rider*.

Before long we are off-road and crossing the paddy fields between villages on ground that looks impassable. The Ural was designed for rough terrain, and we put this to the test a few times. At one stage, we pass some mountain biking tourists who cannot believe what they are seeing. They must have been wondering about the type of mushrooms they'd had in their Pho for breakfast.

The beauty of a side car is not just comfort. Also, as I discover, we have room for a picnic. Stopping in villages along our route, we stock up on local crops of fruit and vegetables and share the odd can of beer. At one place Guan turns the engine off, gets out and starts to push the bike, with me still sitting in the sidecar. I offer to help restart it, but actually he is just showing respect to a funeral ceremony taking place in a village we are passing that grows only kumquats.

All too soon we are headed back to base. Guan says he needs to fix something to do with the engine that I assume is connected with the smoke and the burning oil smell. He drops me outside the hotel and we say our goodbyes. I'm convinced motorcycle and sidecar combination like this one would be a brilliant way to travel across Southeast Asia.

Fourteen: Man Down

Day Twenty-Five, Da Nang, Vietnam
Distance travelled so far: 14,673 km

Hanoi time (GMT +7)

Station	Arrival	Departure
Da Nang		13:15
Tam Ky	14:27	14:30
Quang Ngai	15:30	15:35
Dieu Tri	18:21	18:36
Tuy Hoa	20:11	20:14
Nha Trang	22:04	22:12
Thap Cham	23:40	23:45

Back at Da Nang railway station, the waiting room today is packed as there is both a northbound and a southbound train due here in the next hour. Word comes through that the Saigon (Ho Chi Minh City or HCMC) train has been delayed by an hour, so I settle down next to some Vietnamese aunties who make sure I don't get into any trouble. I have a ticket for SE3, which gets into HCMC early tomorrow morning if all goes well, though I'm learning that it usually doesn't. As time goes by the shouting seems louder, the temperature seems to rise and everything seems

177

harder to achieve. I'm thankful that my new friends fuss around me and feed me sweets.

Because of the delay of the southbound service both trains arrive at the same time, and are reverse-shunted onto the two ends of the same platform. As passengers pour out of the waiting room and onto the platform it would be all too easy to get on the wrong train. A porter is keen to help me for a small fee, but I'm stubborn and determined to manage my own luggage. He's a nice man. Despite my rejection of his services, he still points me to the right place. The two trains are nearly meeting in the middle, and look like one huge train from either side, distinguishable only by the different colours of the carriages. After a quick scrum, I'm on board carriage 11, berth 1. My immediate impression is that the SE3 is a good train. Although it's generally a bit grubby, it has pressed clean white cotton bedding and air conditioning that is working well. This train is painted blue, unlike the colour scheme of all the other state trains. This reminds me of the famous British *Mallard*, which holds the world steam speed record of 126 miles per hour. But in taking over 15 hours to reach Saigon, we certainly won't break any speed records today.

Out in the corridor I notice that the guard has his own small cabin and that the food trolley is much more extensive here too. Unlike the SE1, there are no random women living in cupboards. The Vietnamese version of a samovar is also operational and I check the water temperature to make sure that it is boiling properly. Everything seems in order.

I try to settle in with my new Vietnamese cabin mates, but I'm feeling really tired and have to lie down on my lower berth. There is a small point of sleeper etiquette here, but there are no specific rules. Passengers generally expect to be able to sit on the lower berth during the daytime, so by lying down on my lower berth I'm making another passenger sit somewhere else or climb up to their berth where you can't really sit up. To begin with, the man in question just sits on my bed even though I'm lying down, which is a bit overly familiar, but I'm too tired to care.

I do my best to have a conversation with my cabin mates, but I feel better just lying still and doing nothing. The man I'm sharing with is a medical sales guy heading south to a meeting in Tuy Hoa, and opposite there's a lady and her grand-daughter who are going to see their relatives in Qui Nong. They are all charming, and I'm beginning to actually enjoy sharing a compartment with the locals. It's funny how perspectives change. On an aircraft I hate flying anywhere near kids and family groups, but people don't socialise on planes. On a train you get to talk to people, to swap stories and share food; to learn about the culture of your fellow travellers.

As the day goes on I realise that I'm more than tired; I'm actually unwell and getting worse by the hour. I have no idea why. As I have started to shiver I decide

179

to get my down jacket out of my big bag, despite the energy this absorbs. I try to sleep whilst my fellow travellers sit around me eating instant noodles and fried chicken. The smell makes me retch.

When I mention in passing to the medical sales chap sitting on the end of my bed that I'm not well, he wishes me a speedy recovery after Tet. Tet is the Vietnamese lunar new year. But I can't wait until the Tet festival to feel better, as it is 22 days away.

By sunset I have to declare myself formally on sick parade, and fumble in my bag to find my field first aid box. I take all the pills that I dare, and drink two sachets of rehydration salts at an improvised dilution ratio. My stomach is cramping badly and I can only lie on my back, sweating and shivering at the same time. Time passes in waves of consciousness and passed-out fever.

Waking from weird and colourful hallucinations later in the night I have a strange and urgent feeling that I haven't felt for many years. I'm about to be full on and properly sick. Right now. Shoes on and out into the corridor. Which way? Right I think. Bent over and using every muscle that might be useful in not throwing up, I struggle forwards. Pushing past a businessman, my next obstacle is a woman selling cigarettes and snacks. She doesn't realise what is going to happen until it's too late. I wasn't sure that it was actually going to happen until it did, as you never really know how long you might be able to delay the inevitable. My vomit actually reached as far as the wall behind her, but mainly covers the floor around her. I think I missed her valuable cargo, but couldn't be sure. The look in her eyes was pure horror and disgust, but I don't have time to hang around and apologise. Barging past her I find the toilet mercifully empty and set about filling it with the contents of my stomach. I vomit until there is no more vomit, and then I vomit some more.

Feeling somewhat better, and with no indication of anything more to come up, I step outside the comfort zone of the toilet to witness a full-scale mop up in progress outside. The woman has left the scene of my crime and two carriage attendants are now busy clearing up. It is just as well there are no carpets on this train. I use my best international sign language to apologise and rub my belly with a sad face. I don't know what their words mean, so I retreat into my compartment. I think they might understand.

News of my endeavours have reached my cabin mates before my return. They are actually really nice about it, and maybe now even the sales rep realises I might actually need medical attention before Tet. They must be relieved that I was in a lower berth, as otherwise I might have hosed our compartment down from above rather than the corridor. That would have been a real international incident. With the lights turned off again, I find sleep comes occasionally, though with constant adjustment of the bedding. It's mainly very cold, which nicely balances out my high fever. My main concern now is how I'm going to get off the train, as I feel I can hardly walk, let alone deal with things like bags and tickets.

Day Twenty-Seven, Bien Hoa, Vietnam
Distance travelled so far: 15,329 km

Hanoi time (GMT +7)

Station	Arrival	Departure
Binh Thuan	02:09	02:14
Binh Hoa	04:39	04:42
Saigon	05:20	

The face of my watch is bright green in the near-darkness of the compartment. My watch must be painted with lots of that radioactive lume. It's almost 03:30, and I feel like sitting up for bit. I decide I need some sweet tea and wobble uneasily down to the samovar to get a brew on the go. Unfortunately, this is actually just a warning call from my digestive system. Precisely ten minutes later I feel really sick and head back the toilet to spend another half hour retching and heaving. I haven't eaten for almost 24 hours, but my body is desperate to get rid of whatever it is that is trying to take over my digestive tract. 'Better out than in' is an expression that I can now strongly relate to.

The small window in the toilet is open, and I'm soothed by the damp and cool morning air. The rising sun lifts my mood and my resolve to stop being a lightweight and get back on my feet. The darkness of the night has pandered to my weaker side and now I feel more like fighting on. Fortunately, I don't have much stuff to pack up, and I won't need to hurry off the train as when it stops that is the end of the line. I wonder if I should tip the poor attendants who have had to deal with my mess, but it's academic – they have left the scene and I'm not going to go looking for them.

We chug into the terminus of Saigon's railway station about 20 minutes behind schedule. This is the end of the line, the finishing point of the mythical Reunification Express. Of course, I don't really feel like reflecting on the significance of this right now, more just manoeuvring my luggage down the platform like an asthmatic ant with heavy shopping.

It's only 05:50, but Saigon is already alive with people going about their day's work. I take a chance on a friendly-looking taxi driver with a working meter in his car; we join the traffic and head off down towards the nearby Ben Thang district and my HQ in the city. I'm both amazed and thankful that there is no scam today. I pay him and tip him rather well. I think being an unwell solo traveller makes me appreciate the kindness of others more than I normally do, and perhaps I overcompensate. Outside my hotel the concierge opens the glass doors and I am admitted to paradise – as long as, of course, my credit card is in good working order. I can name just a handful of hotels in the world that are good places to be ill in, and one of them is the Caravelle Hotel in Saigon.

Day Twenty-Eight, Saigon, Vietnam
Distance travelled so far: 15,529 km

If you have ever seen *Apocalypse Now* you will probably remember the scene where Captain Willard is completely drunk in his hotel bedroom. 'Saigon. Shit; I'm still only in Saigon.' Willard is waiting for a mission and is convinced he's getting weaker in his comfy hotel room whilst the enemy are growing stronger in the jungle. 'When I was here, I wanted to be there; when I was there, all I could think of was getting back into the jungle.'

The Caravelle is closely connected to the history of the American war in Vietnam. Staring up at the spinning ceiling fan from my comfy bed, I contemplate that all I would need to become Willard right now is a bottle of Mekong whisky and a few karate lessons. But today I'm not too worried about getting soft in my hotel room, as I know that I will be off on my own mission to Cambodia in just a couple of days.

My speedy recovery has been mainly down to a lovely lady pharmacist who runs a drugstore on nearby Dong Khoi Street. She took a look at me when I arrived and decided I needed some ciprofloxacin and a few other pills to manage the swelling and the pain. It has worked wonders and now I'm almost back to normal. The only lasting symptom seems to be really sore ribs from using muscles to vomit that I haven't had to use in decades.

My suspicion is that I contracted food poisoning from the shellfish I ate the night before travelling, but it might also have been salmonella poisoning from the slightly undercooked egg I had at breakfast before I left Hoi An. I can't prove this, but some of symptoms like tingling lips and shortness of breath suggests to me that it wasn't anything trivial.

I'm feeling well enough to walk now, but I have to be a bit careful as in the fierce heat of southern Vietnam it only takes half an hour walking to sweat a couple of litres of fluids. The traffic is totally mad here, and even though I'm signed off by the Green Cross Man and a practising member of the Tufty Club in the UK, I'm out of my depth here. Earlier, a policeman on a motorbike stopped and escorted me across the road. How embarrassing, and just when I thought I could cross a road like the locals do. The trick is simply to pretend that there is no traffic and keep moving at a steady speed. Everything then just predicts your position and moves around you, but it's a huge leap of faith.

I have been doing some currency swaps today. The banks wouldn't touch some of my money, so I have been doing some trading in the small gold shops you find on most side streets. Russian roubles for Cambodian riel and Chinese yuan for Vietnam dong. I'm a dong multi-millionaire again, but this isn't very impressive and my new wealth will probably not last a single night in the bar at the top of my hotel.

In the evening I'm in a reflective mood. Sipping an imported Krombacher beer in a German bar, I consider the plan for the next few legs of the journey. I have to accept the limitations of the rail network in these parts. Saigon is technically the furthest south that a European can travel to continuously in Asia by rail alone. My journey across Cambodia over the next three days will have to be by bus and car. I understand that a tender is in place to rebuild the Cambodian rail network, but as of today there is pretty much nothing in place. All they have are a few tracks which locals use to guide bamboo carts powered by outboard motors. It sounds like a Cambodian version of the little train in *The Great St Trinian's Train Robbery* (1966).

If all goes well, on Sunday lunchtime I shall catch the Cambodian Express from Aranyaprathet to Bangkok. As soon as I reach Thailand I'm back on the rails for the rest of my journey. But to reach Thailand I'm actually going to have to travel quite a long way north in Cambodia. The reason for this is that there are only a few land border crossing points from Cambodia into Thailand As a result of some longstanding territorial disputes things are 'pretty tense' in places. I think this is coded diplomatic and military language for fighting. My crossing point will be at the infamous Poipet. If what they say about it is true, it's a place I'm not looking forward to visiting.

On the consular front, tomorrow will mark the sixth consecutive visa in my passport. Fingers crossed that like the others it will all work out okay. So far, my forward plan and record keeping has taken the worry out of all the border crossings.

Celebrating fully functioning bowels once again, I try some German sausage for my final meal in Vietnam. This might not be in the spirit of eating as the locals do, but on long trips you need to vary the diet a bit. I'm just happy to have an appetite again. In the bar I discover that I need a password to log onto the internet. I need to check on a few things around my journey from Bangkok to Butterworth. The password is Heinkel. As Basil Fawlty would say, 'Don't mention the war!'

Fifteen: Into the Heart of Darkness

Day Twenty-Nine, Saigon, Vietnam
Distance travelled so far: 15,529 km

Hanoi time (GMT +7)

Bus	Arrival	Departure
Saigon		08:30
Phnom Penh	16:00	

Captain Willard headed upriver by patrol boat to the Do Long bridge on his way to find Colonel Kurtz, but I shall be travelling less tactically and by bus. I found out that there is a river option, but the boat has some drawbacks: you get to choose between sitting for hours in a proper seat (lifejacket provided) next to the engine with all the noise and fumes, or sitting precariously on the cramped open deck in the unrelenting sun. So I have gone for the bus, especially as it allows me to travel more directly point to point towards my objective of Poipet. The similarity in our missions however, is that we are both headed to 'the asshole of the world'.

I didn't want to be late for the bus, so I got up early to find the implausible-looking head office of my bus company, Mekong Express. I have a ticket on the 08:30 bus from Saigon to Phnom Penh. It takes around seven hours to reach Phnom Penh according to the timetable. I have carefully set my expectations for this journey, as there are reports of some very loud Khmer karaoke jamming sessions on board that involve the whole bus and go on for hours. Boarding seems civilised and the seats are even numbered. Today it's mainly Western tourists on board this bus, and things seem pretty relaxed. In place of the karaoke the driver decides to screen some fairly violent Asian movies on the big screen. There is a steward who hands out snacks and points out interesting places along the way – if this were a bus full of Cambodians, I suspect he would become the DJ. I'm choosing my own music today, and top of the playlist is 'Seventeen Seconds' by The Cure.

After nearly three hours we debus at the Vietnamese frontier. The system is very different to my experiences so far on the train. Our bus guide takes all our passports and heads off to Immigration. We then get off without our bags and our names are called one by one at the gate. We then get our passports returned, via the guide, stamped and endorsed. But when they are handed back, mine is missing. No one seems to know what to do about this until, a few minutes later, another bus driver returns with it. That could have gone badly wrong, and I resolve not to let a third party take my passport out of my sight again.

Back on the bus, and then back off the bus again at the Cambodian side of the border. This time I'm using an e-visa which might actually be slower to process than if I had no visa at all. Anyway, after some fingerprinting and stamping, it appears my papers are all in order and I can walk through the frontier post. No one seems to be interested in checking our luggage on either side of the border.

The scenery in Cambodia is subtly different to that in Vietnam. The trees look different, the dogs look different, and there are now rice paddies and lakes everywhere around Highway 1. On the road there are flash cars as well as trashy ones, the result of foreign investment from development programmes.

No one mentioned to me that there was a ship-based section involved in today's trip. Early in the afternoon we drive onto a rather dodgy-looking ferry to cross a lake. The ferry is packed with lorries and we are not allowed off the bus. I think if the ship sank there would be no way out unless you had one of those special hammers. A couple of American backpackers sitting behind me enquire about the availability of lifejackets for the crossing and are disappointed by the answer.

Time passes slowly, and the movies on the television are becoming increasingly gruesome. This is a good bus, but it's not as much fun as travelling by train. Thankfully before too long the fields give way to concrete and we are in the outskirts of Phnom Penh.

At the bus station I recover my bags and secure the services of a tuk tuk. Cambodian tuk tuks are a slightly different species to their Thai and Vietnamese cousins. Here the front of the vehicle is a straightforward moped, attached by a pivot to a wider body for passengers. I guess that it has the advantage of simpler maintenance, but the more integrated style of the Thai version offers more protection and comfort for the driver.

With only one night in town, I decide to visit a few places I knew from my first trip to what was still a war-ravaged country when I first visited Cambodia in 1992. This time I'm driven about by a really nice guy called Kia, who is a Khmer Bob Hoskins, in the sense of *Mona Lisa* (1986). Wherever we stop he waits outside drinking tea whilst I go about my business. I can immediately detect a warmer and more protecting side to Cambodian men than those I came across in Vietnam. In the early evening Kia drops me at the Foreign Correspondents' Club on the banks of the mighty Mekong.

Here I manage to find my usual seat, the one by the window at the end of the bar. The Anchor beer on draft is icy cold and cuts through the humidity of the evening air. The bar is a snapshot of life in the city today. On one side of me a young pony-tailed Cambodian man dressed in shorts and flip-flops drinks a glass of imported white wine whilst smoking a cigarette. On the other side an Australian woman drinks vodka and bores a couple of friends with tales of how important she thinks she is back in the real world. The journalists have now all gone from here, but the club lives on as a good place to share a drink at the end of the day. I will never forget being here back when there were people at the bar reporting live on the heavy fighting with the Khmer Rouge in the North.

Kia spots me before I see him, and prepares the tuk tuk for action. After a look around some of the old bar streets I decide that I need to head back to my hotel and get some rest. There is no time to linger here in Phnom Penh. Tomorrow I'm headed up country to my next staging post, Siem Reap.

Day Thirty, Siem Reap, Cambodia
Distance travelled so far: 16,127 km

Phnom Penh time (GMT +7)

Bus	Arrival	Departure
Phnom Penh		08:30
Siem Reap	15:30	

My day doesn't start particularly well as I manage to miss the first bus to Siem Reap. The Mekong Express office has moved, and no one seems to know where their new place is. When I finally get there, the manager doesn't seem surprised and rebooks me on the next one. No borders today, just a seven-hour run to the town best known for being home to Angkor Wat, the largest religious monument in the world. All is good on the bus, but I don't like their taste in movies and music.

With no borders or river crossings today we make good progress and arrive in the sleepy town of Siem Reap in the early afternoon. At the bus station there is a man from my hotel holding up a handwritten sign for a Mr Ward. When I ask him if he is expecting me he tells me that I'm not on the list, but as there is no Mr Ward here, he will happily take me instead. Once settled in at my hotel I sit by the pool and do my best to ignore a very drunk group of German tourists. I'm used to not going far outside this hotel. On my 1992 trip there were mortar pits dug in each corner of the garden and a rapid reaction force of UN troops in the car park. The nearby religious monuments were nicknamed 'the temples of doom'.

With the map spread out on the bar top I calculate that I have covered around 600km over the last 48 hours on the bus. The Thai border looks close from here, and I have arranged for someone to drive me there in the morning. The only risk that I'm aware of is that the road might not be finished in places, so I need to allow time for minor jungle diversions. It's going to be a busy day and I'm going to need to be as alert as possible to face the infamous touts and scammers of Poipet.

Sixteen: The Cambodian Express

Day Thirty-One, Poipet, Cambodia
Distance travelled so far: 16,277 km

Phnom Penh time (GMT +7)

Car	Arrival	Departure
Siem Reap		09:00
Poipet	11:30	

Bangkok time (GMT +7)

Station	Arrival	Departure
Aranyaprathet		13:55
Bangkok Hua Lamphong	19:55	

Richard, my Cambodian driver, is waiting for me in the reception of the hotel when I arrive to pay my bill. He looks like a veteran of this run and well prepared for the day ahead, dressed in desert combat trousers, a smart short-sleeve shirt and oversized sunglasses. I'm surprised to discover that he drives a Lexus, which makes for a comfortable and fast trip up to the frontier on Highway 6. Our only stop is to pick up some fresh mangosteens. Other than this we speed west, dodging car-sized potholes at over 80 kmh. This two-hour trip used to be an eight-hour trip until a new road was built a few years ago.

Poipet announces its status as a scum-filled frontier town well before you actually reach it. The signs around the highway are no longer trying to advertise things, but instead become warnings about smuggling and the punishments in place for a range of illegal activities. Richard pulls into the car park right by the border point and we get moving before some of the local characters can home in on us. As I get out the car I am surrounded by people appearing from nowhere, offering porterage and transportation services. Shaking hands with Richard, I wonder if he thinks I'm going to make it without getting scammed today. He wishes me good luck and waves as I turn towards the border. I focus on moving forwards and away from the immediate crowd that has formed around the expensive Japanese motorcar. They don't seem hostile, but I suspect they have written books on how to extract every banknote from the wallet of a farang like me. Their gold-toothed smiles seem vaguely menacing, as though just eye contact might result in me being sucked into something. Keeping moving without making eye contact with anyone seems to work well. The only problem with this approach is that after a while I realise that I have been so good at ignoring everyone that I have managed to actually leave Cambodia without getting my passport stamped.

So I'm in no man's land now, a strip of land that, being technically in neither Cambodia nor Thailand, is convenient to the entrepreneurs who have built casinos and cheap hotels here to drain the cash of visiting Thai businessmen. I spot a couple of backpackers by the roadside and compare notes with them. We conclude that I need to go back to Cambodia and get an exit stamp from an immigration office that I have somehow missed. Although by going back to Cambodia this will become a multiple entry, I hope no one will notice my single-entry visa, as I have not yet entered Thailand. No one spots me walking the wrong way as I retrace my steps. The plan works well, and back in Cambodia and after a short queue I give my battered red passport to a man behind a desk that looks to be on its last legs. He looks at my visa and then at me with a slight smile. I wonder if he has some sixth sense to spot visa infringers. He seems content and whacks my passport with a big stamp. I'm officially out of Cambodia. Back into no man's land.

This operation has taken longer than I planned and I could use a public convenience, but of course there are none. I decide my best option is to venture into a casino and park my luggage with a concierge or doorman. Inside the building I enter a dark world where people with wild red eyes smoke a lot and don't seem to notice me. I worry that most are losing more money than they are making, some perhaps all the money that they have in the world. It's not a place to dwell in. I tip the doorman and explain my intentions.

Back out on the road I wheel my bag in and out of the lines of overloaded pick-up trucks towards the bridge and the Thai border building. If Samsonite could see how I was using their bag I think they might decide to commission a whole new series of adverts. The Thai side of Poipet is more organised coming in this direction, and once in a queue there is a vague familiarity with the same forms and procedures you find at an airport. Out of respect for the king I have put on a proper pair of shoes today, and this becomes my first non-plastic-sandals border since Belarus. A few brazen backpackers try to sneak to the front of the queue, but there is a Thai immigration lady who takes personal pride in eliminating queue-barging from this frontier. The guilty people scurry to the back of the line, the woman's vociferous words burning their very souls. Good for her.

When I reach the front, there isn't much interest in either me or my luggage, so after I've waited half an hour, my passport is stamped and I'm in. The overland immigration rules mean that I have just 14 visa-free days to cross Thailand and reach Malaysia. It begins to look like I'm close to making a Poipet home run. Outside of the building I can see the problem for those coming across the other way. You need a visa to enter Cambodia, and that's the perfect cover story for a legion of scammers to set up visa-based services. They mill about outside their shops waiting for the next tourist bus to arrive. Needless to say, they are also very interested in discussing my travel plans. Perhaps a mini-van straight to Pattaya? Haven't I heard that there is no train running to Bangkok today? I hide inside a little ice cream place where I can buy time and get some intel on how to get a taxi to the railway station in Aranyaprathet. Asking for one in the street would spark a fever of excitement amongst the touts, so I play it in the style of an escaping British POW seeking a meeting with the French Resistance. Licking my ice cream methodically before it can fall off its stick in the heat, I ask the woman if she knows anyone. It turns out she speaks English and she does, signalling to someone down the road. Have I been rumbled or saved? A couple of minutes later an unmarked van with dark windows parks outside and out gets a friendly driver. The deal is done before the touts can get to me. It's going to cost just 100 baht (£2) for me and my luggage to the railway station. Wonderful news.

Aranyaprathet station is quiet and lacking in any official activities. A few monks and older ladies with big cloth bags wait on low wooden benches in the shade. The ticket office is closed, but will re-open an hour before the train departs. The platform is a lovely place. Well-maintained flowers grow in beds up and down the platform. A big brass bell hangs outside the station manager's office. Dropping my gear, I sit down with the others and wait. I feel very positive about things. If I can cope with Poipet, then my skills as an adventurer must be improving.

At lunchtime the train from Bangkok arrives. It looks very pretty in the strong sunshine; the saturated colours of the orange train, fluttering flags and the washed effect of the heat haze in an otherwise deep blue sky. Most know it as the Cambodian Express. It doesn't actually reach Cambodia, but its purpose is clear to travellers headed overland out of Thailand.

Quite a few backpackers get off the train and I smile and say hello to some of them. I feel that it's our duty to share news and help those on the route. A few ask me what Poipet was like, and I choose my answers tactfully, as I know what lies ahead for them.

This train will return to Bangkok in a couple of hours. The engine uncouples and reconnects to the other end. I do what the locals do and get my gear onto a carriage, even though I have yet to purchase a ticket. There are no reservations on this train; it's all third class. The logic is to secure a seat on the side of the train that is out of the sun.

The purple and white Thai third-class carriages are all the same on this train. The bench seats are green plastic leatherette, with a matching linoleum floor. Ceiling fans dish out short bursts of refreshing cool breeze before turning to refresh another part of the carriage. The windows are open, but have severe-looking metal shutters, that at first look to me like they are there to keep foreign objects out, but after studying their design, I decide that they are actually ventilated sunshades.

Just as I'm settling in I remember that I have no ticket. Fortunately the station master pulls up the screen at the ticket office counter right on time. We form an orderly queue: monks first, then everyone else. My ticket costs me less than 50 baht (£1) for the seven-hour journey.

After much tooting of the engine horn and ringing of the platform bell, we leave Aranyaprathet. It's a busy train with lots of stops, some not even at stations. The best thing about it is that I'm sitting in a seat next to an open window with the breeze blowing freely in my face for the first time on my journey. Once I'm tired of the noise of life onboard I slip my headphones on and listen to various Peter Gabriel and Kate Bush compilations. Both artists seem to fit my mood perfectly. At this moment I'm absolutely content with life as a rail adventurer. This is what it's all about.

There is lots going on around me. A friendly ticket inspector walks up and down chatting to passengers as he goes. After each and every stop ladies selling kebabs, chicken rice, fruit and shrimp paste pass through. A slightly sinister-looking man wearing a camouflage jacket and aviator sunglasses stands at the end of our carriage. The kids sitting opposite play aimlessly on their android devices. The smell in here is hard to define: strange fruit being peeled, barbecued meat from passing markets and bonfires outside mix with an occasional vegetal stench. I can see the pivotal role of stations here as not just a transport hub but as a community centre for many of the small villages. Life on each platform is fascinating. Occasional random madman chanting, officials dressed in slightly too tightly tailored shirts. Better still, things look ordered, friendly and safe. It's a long time to be sitting on an unpadded plastic seat, but I certainly don't notice this for the first few hours, I'm just enjoying the journey too much.

Our arrival into the urban sprawl of outskirts of Bangkok is subtle at first. Slowly the stations get more modern, motorways pass overhead and before long we weave through the slums that make up some of the least desirable real estate in the city. It's dark outside now, and the novelty of third class and open windows has worn off a little bit. I just want to get to my hotel, but we still have some way to go. Eventually I notice that our line connects with the airport express route, and some passengers switch here to save a journey into downtown Bangkok.

Bangkok Hua Lamphong is an old school station and a delight to use. Rather like the old version of St Pancras in London, inside one enormous curved roof are the platforms, offices and a large space to wait for trains. I need a taxi. I'm not going far, but I find it hard to motivate a driver to take me to my hotel. In the end I wave a bigger banknote about until someone in the line decides to take me.

I'm treating myself to a couple of nights in one of the grand old hotels of Bangkok. Once I'm inside the lobby everything happens in a bit of a whir and in moments I'm escorted to a room that looks out over the busy Chao Phraya river. Captain Willard would be concerned; I could stay here forever getting softer.

My long day finishes with a re-enactment of the sequence at the end of the classic 1958 film *Ice Cold in Alex*. It's the scene where John Mills, Sylvia Syms, Anthony Quayle and Harry Andrews drink glasses of icy Carlsberg beer after surviving crossing the desert in Katy, their Austin ambulance. Waiting for a seat at the hotel bar, I think that it's fair to say that I have a bit of a thirst on. Fortunately I don't have to wait too long, as an Indian lady sits me down at table by the edge of the river, and arranges a supply chain of Singha beers. What a great way to finish another leg of this journey. With over 16,000 km now behind me I'm feeling seriously fulfilled about long-distance rail adventure.

Day Thirty-Two, Bangkok, Thailand
Distance travelled so far: 16,536 km

Without knowing it I have arrived in the eye of a political storm. Overnight things have started to change on the streets and Bangkok is suffering a partial shut-down as the opposition party do their best to oust the caretaking prime minister. There is talk of further action if he does not resign by Wednesday, and the general in charge of the army will not rule out a full-blown coup. I'm planning to be on a train out of here on Tuesday afternoon, as long as I can get back to the railway station.

The duty manager has advised me not to travel far away from the lobby today. I wonder what their contingency plan is if things get difficult outside. I rather suspect that the men in very dark suits here have a good one. Perhaps a helicopter evacuation from the roof, or a big boat down the river. From my room I can see protesters forming a blockade on a nearby road bridge. They are armed with just flags and whistles, and I can see no violence. They are mobile, travelling on bikes and mopeds, and they move on before there is any confrontation.

I have almost forgotten that I don't yet have any tickets for my next journey when a man arrives at my door with an envelope from my agent in Bangkok. I now have a ticket on tomorrow's International Express or Special Express, bound for Butterworth in Malaysia. This is the only Thai train that leaves the country, hence its name. My ticket shows that I have a sleeper reservation in second class, and a lower berth as well, just as I had asked for. Throughout this journey I have come to rely on local agents getting me the right tickets and delivering them to me when I arrive in new places. This approach has been really effective and it has been great to know someone is looking after things in the next port of call.

On paper the train looks to be a good one, but the timetable hides a small but significant risk. During the night it crosses a troubled part of southern Thailand where a separatist movement has killed thousands, and past incidents have included bombing of both the rail line and the railway station at Hat Yai. Martial law is still in place to try to supress the almost daily attacks. The train now has armed protection on board, but it is still seen by the Foreign and Commonwealth Office as a route to avoid if possible. As a long-range rail adventurer I have to take calculated risks, and this is one that I must take if I want to stay on the tracks.

The Chao Phraya river changes character at night. The barges towing sand downriver moor up, and in their place the river fills with brightly lit cruise boats offering dinner and a dance to partygoers. High up from the vantage point of my hotel room I can see them passing up- and downstream in well-choreographed manoeuvres between the spans of the bridges. The passengers seem to be having a good time, oblivious to what else might be going on back on dry land. I decide to play it safe, and dine in my room. Quite what I'm expecting to happen I'm not sure, but this is also an excuse for a cheese fest. I have developed a serious cheese craving over the past few weeks, so tonight I have managed to organise a self-assembled cheese board and a bottle of reasonable wine from a nearby supermarket. So much for a big night out in Bangkok.

Day Thirty-Three, Bangkok, Thailand
Distance travelled so far: 16,536 km

Bangkok time (GMT +7)

Station	Arrival	Departure
Bangkok Thonburi		07:50
Kanchanaburi	10:25	10:35
River Kwae Bridge	10:44	
River Kwae Bridge		14:40
Kanchanaburi	14:45	14:48
Bangkok Thonburi	17:40	

The word on the street is that the protesters have said they will not be targeting the railways. With this in mind I have decided to ignore the general warnings of my hotel and take the train back to the River Kwae for a day. This train is not on my route to Singapore, but I'm really keen to be able to connect *A Bridge Too*

Far to *Bridge on the River Kwai* as part of this journey. To achieve this I have to head north west of Bangkok, in the direction of Myanmar. It's an early start, and I take the boat upriver to the Thonburi station pier in the pre-dawn gloom. The old station, a short walk from the pier, is now hidden behind an enormous new hospital.

Train 257 is the first one of the day from Bangkok to the River Kwae and on to Nam Tok. It is already sitting on the main platform but without an engine. Once I have my ticket I climb aboard and settle down for the three-hour run up to the river. This is a third-class train, identical to the one I travelled on from the Cambodian border. It slowly fills up with a mixture of travellers and locals. There are no real tourists here, as they will all be on bus tours, no doubt stopping off at many gem shops and silk factories en route.

I doze intermittently, waking only for the train horn and occasional ticket inspections. It's quite liberating not having any luggage with me today. I must try this more often. We reach the war graves of Kanchanaburi on time, then it's just a short hop to the station at the river itself where I get off and watch the train cross the bridge and slip out of sight on the other bank.

My only purpose here today is reflection on past events. I'm a great believer in the sense of place. I decide to cross the bridge to reach the quieter surroundings of the western bank of the river. The

206

curved spans date back to 1943, but the straight ones are more modern, built after the bridge had been hit by an American bomb in 1945. At several places there are passing points where people can get out of the path of the oncoming trains, and I wonder how often tourists have a near miss with a locomotive.

I have time to think about my journey here, to think about the connection of the bridges that I have crossed and to think about the sacrifice made by the men who died building and sometimes fighting over them. Arnhem feels a long way away, but I have travelled by train between these two bridges in just 31 days. During my lifetime, the stories of these places have left living memories; a sad but inevitable passing of time.

Feeling that I have made my connection with the bridge I walk along the banks for a couple of hours before catching the 258 service back to Bangkok in the afternoon. The more time I spend on these third-class trains the more I like them. Open windows are a bit of a thrill, and the locals are nearly all very friendly.

Back in Bangkok the streets still seem calm, but I'm not sure how well I can read the situation. As long as I can reach Hua Lamphong station tomorrow, then I'm bound for Butterworth, Malaysia.

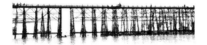

Seventeen: Disco Nights

Day Thirty-Four, Bangkok, Thailand
Distance travelled so far: 16,632 km

Bangkok time (GMT +7)

Station	Arrival	Departure
Bangkok		14:45
Sam Sen	14:58	15:00
Bang Sue Junction	15:06	15:09
Bang Bamru	15:23	15:26
Sala Ya	15:40	15:43
Nakhon Pathom	16:08	16:11
Rachaburi	16:58	17:01
Phetchaburi	17:45	17:47
Hua Hin	18:40	18:45
Bang Saphan Yai	21:04	21:07
Chumphon	22:41	22:45

Arriving back at Hua Lamphong the following lunchtime, I immediately notice a difference about the place. There is now a resident population of a few thousand protesters living inside the station concourse. Their political allegiance is clear, as they wear red shirts, the colour of the United Front for

Democracy against Dictatorship. Everyone is well behaved and I can't see a single soldier here. Sitting on the floor, they are calm and chatty, waiting for instructions on where they are to move to.

My train is already up on the departures board; the Special Express, platform number 5 at 14:45. It is pretty easy to spot, as it is the only train that leaves Thailand. I'm surprised to find that there is no security here, no ticket check, and I'm free to wander onto the platform and find my carriage. The train is also serving a number of domestic stations, and further down the line there are jumping-off points for those in search of Thailand's southern islands. Just two second-class sleeper carriages will then cross the frontier and continue down to Butterworth. I'm in one of those: coach 3, berth 18.

On the outside, the carriages are mostly painted Thai Railways purple, but parts of the skin are unpainted polished panels of riveted aluminium, which give the train a 1950s Airstream look. The coaches were originally Korean and their functional design inside is open plan but comfortable-looking. Pairs of wide seats face each other at either end of the windows on each side of the carriage. At night the seats are pulled together to become one lower berth, and a second berth hinges down from the ceiling. The lower berth is actually a little wider, and costs an extra few hundred baht. My lower berth ticket cost 1,210 baht (£22) for a 23-hour journey. I think I actually paid more than the ticket price, just to get it issued early and delivered to my hotel, but it's still a great deal.

Delighted that the air conditioning seems to work well, I set up my home at seat 18. I'm in the middle of the coach, something I have learned is a good position, as it tends to offer a smoother ride and at the same time is well away from the toilets and the smokers. My only concern is the passenger opposite me in seat 17, who hasn't arrived yet, and I'm having to use that seat as a luggage store as there is no room for my big bag anywhere else in the coach. By chance I have the only seat on the train with a power socket next to it, and immediately I am the go-to guy for power. I get the job of supervising the charging of dozens of mobile devices as the carriage fills up.

Breaking the mould for most Thai people, the carriage supervisor is completely miserable. He has been no help at all with my luggage problem, but at least he hasn't thrown my bag off yet. We eventually get going about 15 minutes late, and I'm feeling better about this train as I settle in. It's cool, and the atmosphere is calm and friendly on board. There are people moving up and down selling all sorts of stuff, but unless you speak Thai, much of it is unrecognisable.

As the afternoon goes on I seem to have most of the phones charged, and a stream of happy passengers visit me to pick them up again. I discover that the guard is in fact okay, and like most young Thai people, speaks a little English when pushed. My theory is that he perhaps wishes he was in the army, and is practising looking as hard as he possibly can. He tells me that if the passenger in seat 17 turns up, I can just put my bag in the corridor instead. On a train back home, that would cause an international incident. Another official, who I assume to have the job of purser, offers me meals at my seat. I'm going to take dinner in the restaurant, but for tomorrow morning I pre-order a full Thai breakfast with coffee in bed.

It's not much longer until I'm in train travel nirvana. The sun is setting, the purser has brought along to me a big bottle of icy Chang beer and shown me the menu, which helpfully has lots of little coloured pictures of all the dishes on offer. He even stops by to top up my glass every so often. This feels more like first class to me. I have the discovery edition of *Dark Side of the Moon* up loud on my headphones whilst I admire the emerging new landscape of jungle, coconut trees, little mountains and steep cliffs.

I have been observing the crew on this train, and their roles seem quite specialised. Our slightly miserable carriage guard inspects tickets, looks as hard as he can, and walks up and down a lot. He makes up the bunks, wears a white shirt and carries a whistle. The carriage security man looks after immigration and has lots of paperwork with him. He wears a brown shirt and carries a .38 pistol on his belt. The carriage purser takes orders, deals with the restaurant, and serves you at your seat. He wears an orange shirt and always carries a menu. Finally, there is carriage cleaner. He wears a blue shirt and always has a broom to hand. He takes his job very seriously and the bathrooms are kept immaculate in this carriage. It's important to know the split of responsibilities here as it's a waste of time asking the security guy for a beer, or the purser for an immigration form.

Down the corridor and through to the car next door is the restaurant carriage. It's called the Bogie Restaurant, and that's trainspeak, not anything nasal. With the purser doing such a good job, I almost missed the restaurant carriage and I am pleased I didn't. It's full of life, teeming with real characters. My four-course dinner here costs 220 baht (£4.50). Better still, there is a complimentary accompaniment of lively Thai rock music and the offer of a karaoke session later.

Just to spice up my dinner even more, a charming but strangely tall woman sits down opposite me at my table, and I'm fairly sure she's a ladyboy. I do my best to look relaxed and friendly, but it's all too much for my repressed English sensibilities, so I make my excuses and head back to carriage 3 for early bed and no karaoke. That might be for everyone's benefit, as other than a few very particular songs from the Andy Williams back catalogue I'm dreadful at singing.

By the time I return to my seat the purser has made it into a bed and put my big bag in the corridor where people seem to be managing to get past it okay. I decide that staying awake isn't going to lessen the very small risk of the train being hijacked or derailed by an explosion, so I lie down on the surprisingly comfy mattress and pull my curtain closed.

Day Thirty-Five, Hat Yai, Thailand
Distance travelled so far: 17,755 km

Bangkok time (GMT +7)

Station	Arrival	Departure
Hat Yai	06:20	06:35
Padang Besar	09:00	10:25
Arau	10:40	10:44
Sungai Petani	11:40	11:42
Bukit Maertajam	12:02	12:05
Butterworth	12:16	

I'm up fairly early the next morning, as the Thai restaurant carriage will turn back for Bangkok well before we get to the Malaysian border. Noticing that I'm up and so is the passenger above me, Mr Grumpy converts our sleepers back to seats and refits the bedding in the space above the top bunk. The purser then sets up a small table in front of me and tells me that my breakfast is on the way. There have been no problems in the night. My only issue was using the toilet, which is so wet inside with regular hose-downs that it might have a leech problem. I wish I had bothered to unpack my plastic sandals.

At 07:30 we arrive at Hat Yai Junction, a reminder that we are now in the heart of bandit country. I can't see much military activity around the station, but there is a lot of fried chicken being loaded on board our train from a catering trolley on the platform. I hope all those chickens didn't die needlessly. I always used to think that stations called junctions sounded quite glamorous: I must have been thinking of Bhowani rather than Watford.

The shortened train, with just three carriages and armed guards, departs from here for the border just before 8.00 am. Using flawed tactical thinking I decide that this is good, as if someone was going to attack us they would surely do it in the night, or possibly at dawn. The train makes a comforting rat-a-tat-tat noise along the elderly rails, and there is now a purring sound from the small diesel engine pulling us down the line. Then without warning a screech of brakes, a massive judder and a violent stop. Is it an ambush? But there is no gunfire, and I can't see anyone outside. My guard seems to have some idea of what is going on, and for some reason he wants to get up onto the roof of the train to be sure. If I spoke Thai I might get a rolling update on news relayed from the roof, but instead I have to wait for the official verdict on our predicament. Those sitting around me don't seem to be panicking, so I sit back and wait like this happens to me every day at Hat Yai. Elephants on the line again, no doubt.

It's not long before our fate is confirmed, as long as you speak Thai. Our carriage is apparently unserviceable and the train will be leaving it behind; something to do with the brakes or the hydraulics. There is a mass exodus into the next carriage, and I follow, not wanting to be left behind in bandit country with only fried chicken to defend myself. I'm now a refugee in carriage 3, and I wonder where it is headed. I'm not sure that the whole train goes to Butterworth, so I try to enquire about our destination. The guard here wears earphones so you can't communicate with him. I suspect he's secretly rocking to some Red Hot Chili

Peppers whilst he goes about his job.

Once my bags are installed in the right part of the train I walk down to the end of the coach and peer out of the open door to see what is happening to our crippled carriage. The tracks are covered in muck and litter, and a few metres down the line the uncoupled broken carriage is in the process of being hauled away by a local shunter.

Soon our now two-carriage train is under way again, destination Padang Besar, right at the frontier. Time to swap my baht for ringgit with a man sitting opposite me. He doesn't look like a currency trader, and once we have finished our business I chat with him, as he speaks pretty good English. He turns out to be an off-duty train driver, and an ideal person to be sitting near in the event that we lose any more carriages. Padang Besar is a bit different to every other rail border that I have so far encountered on this journey. They want us off the train, and with all our luggage. It's a short walk through the Malaysian formalities, a turning off the platform into a one-way system of little rooms. The usual stamping of passports, and no visa is needed for me this time. It's good to be visiting a Commonwealth country. Strangely there is no paperwork either, and I have no idea why, especially given its colonial past, as Britain invented red tape. The Customs people do a full search of my bags; I must look a bit dodgy, or more likely just unlike all the other passengers. A lady wearing a hijab peers at the image of my bag on the x-ray and decides that further investigation is required. I get the bag unlocked and let them poke around. The only thing that seems to interest them is my first aid box which contains hypodermic needles and scalpels, all in sterile packaging. Clearing me of being a drug user, they tell me it's all okay.

With this all done we are back through a little door and out onto the same platform once again. Our train is in the same place. I assume they have searched it, but I haven't seen them do this. A rather clapped-out-looking silver KTM locomotive is being attached to our two carriages, ready to take us south to Butterworth. There is a new guard on the train, and he welcomes me to Malaysia.

It's not very far to Butterworth, and once I remember to adjust my watch to GMT +8, I realise that we have arrived at the railhead in no time. Butterworth is not on the main north–south line, but is the city that connects mainland Malaysia to the tropical island of Penang, and it seems rude not to stop off here for a little break. All I have to do is carry my bags a short distance out of the station and up a ramp and ahead of me is the ferry to Georgetown. Cost RM1.20 (30p), return.

It's a strange feeling to have travelled this far and to know that my final objective is now less than a day away by train. More reason not to have to hurry, and perhaps for the first time it sinks in that unless something goes badly wrong, I shall soon be a veteran of the UK–Singapore run. But for now, I can forget all about trains, tickets, connections and red tape. That is until I remember that I'm doing an interview with someone about train travel this evening.

Eighteen: The Penang Club

Day Thirty-Six, Penang, Malaysia
Distance travelled so far: 17,973 km

My base in Penang is the Eastern & Oriental Hotel which was founded by the Sarkies Brothers in 1885, and once described as the finest hotel east of Suez. It is a past home to many very well-known people, including two of my heroes, Kipling and Conrad. *Apocalypse Now* was based on Conrad's novel *Heart of Darkness*, and Kipling wrote *The Man Who Would Be King*, which later became a brilliant 1975 film.

If I spent very long here I would begin to think Great Britain still had an empire. I only wish I had packed a Panama hat and linen jacket, or better still, a pith helmet. The hotel even provides me with a batman with a black bow tie who calls himself Adam. He is simply charming, and I'm sure would take care of anything I asked of him. But I don't have time to put his skills to the test, as I'm being shown around this evening by Ian, a British expat writer.

Dinner is hawker centre style, washed down with icy Tiger. After a tour round town, Ian invites me back to the Penang Club for a drink, where we discuss my trip for an article he is writing. Ian is into the possibility of big rail journeys, so it's a good chance to compare notes. The Penang Club was established in 1868 as an expat enclave in a very Victorian sort of a way. It retains this feel today, albeit now amidst a very different Penang.

My interview is the first I have given about the trip, and I'm unprepared for some of his questions. It's easy to answer timetable and route questions: I reckon I'm good enough for *Mastermind* or *University Challenge* on subjects such as the Siberian rail network or naming Chinese provinces by pictures of their outline alone. But the big questions tonight are 'why?' and 'what next?'. I have to explain that I don't yet have an answer for 'what next?', but I do try and explain 'why?'. After a few overly long attempts, I decide to simplify the answer for his tape recorder. I find it fulfilling and it makes me happy. Ian gives me an appreciative smile; I suspect he feels the same way about train travel.

Much later, when I get back to the E&O, I contemplate going for a nightcap in Farquhar's Bar, but decide against it for fear that I would not be able to stop myself saying things like 'Stop throwing those bloody spears at me!' to the barman. I manage to walk on past the bar and take the lift up to my room. It's time for some well-earned rest.

Over the next few days I recharge the batteries and mix with people who travel between countries and continents by pressurised jet aircraft. I'm sure that will never catch on. I keep hearing people in bars complaining about their airline's upgrade policy, and then I get asked which airline I used to get here. It feels strange to do nothing, but other than attending a spot of cookery school I hang around the pool or the beach, playing at being a tourist. My diet in Penang revolves around chicken biryani, a dish which is really popular in these parts and reflects the ethnicity and tastes of the locals living here. It is so delicious that I go so far as to learn how to make a weapons grade biryani. My teacher encourages me with his holistic thinking. 'Keep stirring, keep smiling,' he says all the time. Then he insists I do a little dance to a well-known Beyoncé song as we mash up fresh curry paste. I decide that cookery school is like rail travel; it gets you to just enjoy living in the moment.

It's not long, though, before I feel that I want to get back on the rails. Penang is a nice island, but it is punishingly expensive where I am staying, and somehow lacks the feeling of authenticity that I have had through the last few countries in my journey. I brief Adam of my plans and he makes arrangements for my departure. He offers to pack my bags, but I don't think that would be fair on him.

Day Thirty-Eight, Butterworth, Malaysia
Distance travelled so far: 18,027 km

Kuala Lumpur time (GMT +7)

Station	Arrival	Departure
Butterworth		07:33
Ipoh	09:18	09:22
Kuala Lumpur	11:15	11:58
Palau Sebang	13:40	13:46
Gemas	14:52	14:55
Kluang	17:00	17:06
Johor Bahru	18:40	18:45
Singapore Woodlands	22:00	

I'm up early for my trip on the Rakyat Express, my last big train of this journey. Adam provides me with a packed breakfast, and the pith-helmet-wearing concierge drives me down to the ferry terminal. I wait there in the gloom with other commuters for the first ferry of the day to Butterworth. The timings of the first ferry are somewhat imprecise, so I have had to allow plenty of time to make the departing train to Singapore at 07:33. Just when I'm thinking that if there is no ferry soon I might have to swim for it, the lights of the boat shine into the covered dock of the terminal building. Loading takes ten minutes, and we cast off in the swell and head back in the direction of the mainland. In the distance I can just make out the lights on the huge Penang Bridge that connects the island to the mainland by road.

At first there isn't much to see on the platform at Butterworth. No trains, and just a few intrepid tourists with packed breakfasts like mine, who have decided to take the train to Kuala Lumpur (KL) today rather than flying. Dawn gently breaks and then the single headlight of Train Number 1 is visible in the distance as it approaches from the main line. A health-and-safety-obsessed station guard keeps us all well away from the train until the locomotive has been successfully connected. I show him my camera, and he lets me pass to do my stuff at the front end of the train. I'm not sure if there are many trainspotters in Malaysia, as he looks a little puzzled.

Most of the stations on this route seem to be brand new, made of steel and concrete that is just a few months old. But the trains are still mainly old and decrepit. Our loco today is a small silver-painted engine with a major rust problem. It looks knackered. It is hooked up to ten carriages, mainly second-class. They all turn out to be Korean, built by Hyundai. I'm travelling in the single first-class carriage which is connected to a restaurant carriage in front of the second-class coaches. These are newer and a bit nicer-looking than the one I'm in. I contemplate downgrading, but this would almost certainly cause a seat reservation crisis, so I stick where I am for the time being. My seat has seen better days: the foam from underneath the heavily soiled fabric is exposed, and has been eaten away by something. The layout here is two seats on one side, and a single row on the other, so at least it's not cramped. There is a luggage rack at one end in the corridor and a toilet at the other that I would rate as only suitable for emergencies. A powerful air conditioning system chills the carriage down to a temperature suitable for storing fresh food.

The journey today is going to take around 14 hours and we are due to arrive at Singapore Woodlands at 22:00 tonight, assuming all goes to plan. In many ways this is my least favourite type of train trip. It is too short a journey to really settle in, like on an overnight train, but rather too long a journey for a day trip. Anyway, this is my home for the day, so I need to make the best of what I have. It looks like most passengers in my carriage are going to Ipoh or KL, just a few hours away. The guard inspects my ticket and smiles at me as if to recognise that he's got a madman on his hands. He tells me I'm going to be here for the day. I nod and smile back like a rail-obsessed lunatic.

Slightly late, the little diesel engine revs up, and black oily smoke billows out of its funnel. There is some flag waving, whistle blowing and tooting of the horn before we finally we trundle out of Butterworth and rejoin the main southbound line. I'm a little bored after just half an hour, so I open my packed breakfast to add a dimension of excitement to the morning. Have I lost my train mojo? Maybe I should have just travelled to KL today.

By the time we arrive in KL I have eaten my breakfast, finished the crossword in yesterday's *Straits Times* and completed and refiled all the paperwork alphabetically in my office folder. Everyone gets off here apart from me and a family at the other end of the carriage. Staff come on board to clean the train, and outside they even wash the windows. The carriage quickly fills up with a Taiwanese tour group, and we are on the move again in under 15 minutes.

Seeking something to do, and not speaking any passable Taiwanese, I opt for a late lunch from the trolley service. I go for fried rice and sweet black coffee, which costs RM 8 (£1.49). I eat this whilst listening to 'Tubular Bells II' by Mike Oldfield. The day continues to pass slowly. The sun very gradually arcs towards the western horizon with the passing of time. At just after 16:00 we pull into a place called Pulau Sebang, and in the space of a minute I find myself alone in the carriage. There must be something culturally significant here that I don't know about. So now I'm not just bored, but lonely too. I spend the rest of the afternoon reading and writing notes in my journal.

Eventually at around 21:00 we arrive at Johor Bahru Central station, and a Malaysian immigration officer hops on board to check travel documents. This is the frontier town perched across the Johor Strait from Singapore. He is lacking a briefcase, so he just hand-writes an exit note in green ink in my passport and returns it to me in the manner of a schoolmaster who has just marked some substandard homework. Green ink was the sign of poor results on my school record card, and the colour haunts me to this day.

From here the train crosses the long causeway bridge where it connects with Woodlands CIQ, the station on the northern side of the island state that is Singapore. This is a fairly new arrangement, and the end of the line. It is sadly no longer possible to travel as far south as the wonderfully colonial Tanjong Pagar station on Keppel Road.

There is a brief moment for me to reflect on the history of this part of the island. During the Battle of Singapore, the Imperial Japanese Army led by General Yamashita could not use this causeway as it had been intentionally blown up by the Allies. Instead he committed his armies to assault by barge to the western side of the causeway, the opposite route from the one that they had been expected to use. This was the beginning of the Fall of Singapore, and on 15th February 1942, the largest ever surrender in British military history took place on the island. Over 80,000 Allied soldiers became prisoners of war, and many were transported to work on the Death Railway. One of the prisoners was a 22-year-old man by the name of Lieutenant Eric Lomax.

The process at Woodlands CIQ is just like being at an airport. The only problem is that I have forgotten what you do at airports – I just now know very well how it works at railway stations. I try to look smart and approach an immigration guard standing at a half-height booth. As I hand him my passport he asks me for my documents. Documents? How embarrassing, I need to fill in an entry card and a Customs declaration and no one has given them to me. He points me to a place where naughty people like me go to complete the documents that they should have arrived with. I try again and this time with a heavy stamp, I'm in. He offers me a sweet, and smiles. This is by far the nicest smile I have seen at a land immigration point over the entire journey.

Everything is so regulated in Singapore that I don't have to worry about a taxi scam. There is a regulated queue of well-maintained blue and yellow metered cars. Soon we are bombing down the Bukit Timah Expressway towards downtown Suntec City. I haven't seen skyscrapers like this since Beijing, and I'm mesmerised by the size of the multi-lane roadways. My driver seems to be using his impressive satnav to see ahead rather than the traditional view out the windscreen. With all the coloured lights on his device it does look a bit like a computer game.

At the hotel there is no red carpet to greet me, but they seem to treat all their guests like VIPs. A duty manager welcomes me and escorts me to my room. When he opens the room door I realise that I have been upgraded to a big suite. The bathroom is the size of a squash court. I have much business to conduct in there, but it will have to wait until I have had a beer.

Outside the hotel it is hot and humid, but now late in the evening it is not too oppressive, so I decide to sit outside a nearby tapas bar for my celebratory beverage. It's a special drink, most memorable perhaps from its stunning price, the costliest beer of my trip. Singapore has become an expensive city, and

I have become too used to the cheapness of street food and beer in other, less developed, parts of Asia.

Today's train journey hasn't been my favourite one, and it's perhaps a shame that my last journey wasn't more satisfying. I feel an incredible high that I have achieved what I set out to do, but then with that comes the sinking feeling that my amazing journey is almost over and I will soon have to revert to normality. But this evening is my chance to reflect on what I have done, albeit with some rapidly appearing rose-tinted spectacles. Two beers later, and I can't resist telling someone where I have come from. A German lady perhaps senses something different about me. She asks me what I'm doing here. I assume it's a chat-up line for networking and doing business in the city, so when I tell her my story she insists I join a group of her friends. I find myself quite enjoying telling stories of fire engines, bunkers, weird food and mad borders. I discover that I quite like talking about my adventures. In fact, I'm still there talking about them at closing time, and my audience has grown.

Back in my room, or one of the rooms that make up my room, I phone down to order some room service, as I have forgotten to eat anything since getting off the Rakyat Express. But I manage to fall asleep on the sofa before the food arrives, and have to be woken up by the duty manager on the phone. I probably sound a bit washed-out. 'Are you all right?' he asks me. 'Of course I am,' I tell him. 'Just a little tired from my 18,700 km train journey.' It is only at that moment that I really consider how washed out I must be. I'm seriously tired, not just from today's journey, but from nearly six weeks of rail adventure.

Nineteen: The Sentosa Express

Day Thirty-Nine, Sentosa Island, Singapore
Distance travelled so far: 18,703 km

Singapore time (GMT +)

Station	Arrival	Departure
VivoCity		10:30
Sentosa	10:38	

There is actually another rail line that extends south of Singapore. You won't find it listed as one of the great railway journeys in the world. Opened in 2007, it connects Singapore to the resort island of Sentosa. I decide that I want to add this to my journey for two reasons. Firstly, that someone is bound to point it out to me when I get back home, and secondly, that it allows me to visit the ruins of Fort Siloso, the British gunnery base on the island. So today I'm travelling a further two kilometres south, and over one final unnamed rail bridge.

The monorail was actually first constructed in the 1980s, but demolished to make way for the faster version with fewer stops that runs today. First of all I need to catch an MRT train down to Harbourfront station to reach it. You can't help but admire Singapore's mass transit system. It's clean, cheap and efficient, and it runs on time. After emerging from the escalators into the vast temple of retail therapy known as VivoCity, it's a short walk to reach the departure point of the Sentosa Express.

The station is fairly unique and you can't miss this particular train. Once you have a ticket, up on the platform you meet staff who are trained to look happier than you might think is reasonably possible. Passengers queue behind roped-off areas, awaiting the arrival of the next train. It's not long before the sleek front end of the train comes into view, and the most stinking thing about it is its colour. It is painted bright purple. This doesn't look like the stuff of hard core long-range rail adventure, but I'm up for it. The double door slides open, the staff invite us to board and the carriages fill up with tourists, families and migrant workers having a well-earned day off. Once the doors are closed the staff all wave manically at the passengers and we glide off towards Sentosa at about 30kph. Inside of the train there are a few simple plastic bench seats and a few pictures of pirates conveying information about the five-minute journey in English, Chinese and Japanese.

Reaching the main station in Sentosa, I find a bus to take me up the hill to Fort Siloso on the western tip of the island. The base was built by the British army in the 1880s, and much of it is well preserved but ignored by most visitors to the island who are seeking the thrills of Universal Studios or the casino. The gun battery saw action in the Fall of Singapore, although it was not very effective at stopping the Japanese advance, as its shells were designed to penetrate the armour of ships attacking from the south rather than soldiers advancing from the north.

I'm alone here on a concrete gun emplacement looking out over the Singapore Strait to the outlying islands of the Indonesian archipelago. Without much warning there are thunderclaps overhead, and the afternoon rains begin. Rain at this latitude isn't something that gently materialises like in the United Kingdom. Here the very definition of 'the heavens opening' is appropriate, and all I can do is duck under the nearby corrugated metal shelter over the gun's firing point and wait for the storm to pass. Under here I am covered from the stair rods of rain and the splattering of the earth around my position. It actually feels good to be isolated from everyone else; maybe this is a proxy for solo travel by train, and I'm not yet quite ready to enter back into everyday society.

From my tactical viewpoint I can see not just the Singapore Strait, but I can also look back towards the main island, where lightning bolts now collide with the tops of the residential skyscrapers of neighbouring Boon Lay. My attention is suddenly drawn by movement above, not of the lightning flashes, but of a wriggling snake; a long, thin, bright green snake. It is hanging down from one the poles of the corrugated roof uncomfortably close to where I am sheltering. I hate snakes. Give me deadly spiders or vicious tigers any day – just not snakes. People often say that snakes are scared of humans and will usually retreat, but 30 seconds pass and I experience no such luck. It drops out of the roof and heads across the gravel and concrete floor to the entrance, from where it stares at me. My shelter from the rain has now become a temple of doom!

Hindsight is a wonderful thing, but I wish I had taken some snake identification lessons at some point in the past. Don't panic, Matthew, it's probably harmless, I tell myself. It doesn't look big enough to strangle me, but could it be a spiting, biting type of venomous snake? A pit viper, a Malayan krait, or maybe even a coral snake? Reviewing my options, I could remain here until the snake goes away, or alternatively I could jump around it and escape up the trench towards the freedom of the surface. I decide to wait it out for half an hour; just me and the snake sheltering from the torrential rain. With time on my side I consider another option. I could phone the police. Maybe they have a snake specialist or even a reptile department? On reflection I decide this sounds a bit lame, and I don't wish to become the laughing stock of the Royal Geographical Society. What would Percy Fawcett do?

The snake makes a slight move over to one side of the path and I make a sudden and irrevocable decision. The flow of adrenaline makes me perform like an Olympic triple jumper, and my fat frame bounds across the gun position in the direction of the upward sloping trench. I run for safety without looking back, and for good measure shout 'Snaaaake!'

quite loudly as I exit the pit. I'm soaked to the skin in seconds, the time it takes me to reach another bunker. This one is occupied by a park warden who assures me that it was probably only a tree snake. He even points to a sign warning of the potential dangers of snakes here, something I'd failed to notice on the way in.

From my new bunker I have a better view of Singapore and once I have looked around I sit down and wait for the rains to pass. Through the vegetation here I can see the sea and the first few islands of the Indonesian archipelago. Tax free beer is only ten or so kilometres away. But to travel any further south from here you need a ship. I always liked the idea of this journey progressing to Australia, but there is no obvious way of doing that. A new set of skills would be needed to master the work of shipping agents and a passage on a commercial vessel bound to Darwin via the Java Sea. I doff my cap to those that have done that, but for me this 18,703 km trip has been enough of an adventure for the time being.

With my train journey over I spend a few days hanging round expat-type bars on Boat Quay, drinking very cold beer. The final bridge that I have to cross is the Cavenagh Bridge, which neatly allows me to cut across the river and back to my hotel. Over at nearby Raffles Hotel I hear that in 1902 they shot a tiger in the billiard room. The only tigers I'm dealing with during my stay are out of a frosted glass. It's time to go home and work out whereabouts on the planet I will travel to next - by train, of course.

The Trains (and other transport)

Leg 1
From Newcastle to Ijmuiden and Amsterdam
DFDS ferry *King Seaways*, then bus
401 km, 17 hours

Leg 2
From Amsterdam to Warsaw
EN447 *Jan Kiepura*
1,094 km, 16 hours

Leg 3
From Warsaw to Moscow
D10 *Polonez*
1,502 km, 20 hours

Leg 4
From Moscow to Beijing (Trans-Mongolian)
Train 004
10,823 km, 6 days

Leg 5
From Beijing to Hanoi
T5 train
2,995 km, 3 days

Leg 6
From Hanoi to Da Nang
SE1 train
763 km, 15 hours

Leg 7
From Da Nang to Saigon
SE3 train
961 km, 15 hours

Leg 8
From Saigon to Phnom Penh
Mekong Express bus
240 km, 7 hours

Leg 9
Phnom Penh – Siam Reap
Mekong Express bus
314 km, 6 hours

Leg 10
From Siam Reap to Bangkok
Car to Poipet, then the Cambodian Express
407 km, 11 hours

Leg 11
From Bangkok to Butterworth
Train 35 International Express
926 km, 23 hours

Leg 12
From Butterworth to Singapore
Train 1 Rakyat Express
1,058 km, 14 hours

Total planned trip duration: 45 days
Total planned trip distance: 18,440 km

The Bridges

Forth Rail Bridge, Edinburgh, Scotland

This iconic bridge crossing the Firth of Forth at South Queensferry is a designated UNESCO world heritage site. When opened by the future Edward VII in 1890, it was the longest single cantilever span bridge in the world. The Forth Bridge has appeared in several films, perhaps most famously in *The 39 Steps*. Edinburgh was my home at the time of embarking on this adventure, and also home to author Eric Lomax until 1939.

John Frost Bridge, Arnhem, Netherlands

The modern-day road bridge over the Lower Rhine in the Netherlands was named the John Frostbrug in 1977, the original bridge having been bombed by the Allies in 1944 and replaced by an identical bridge in 1948. Although the original bridge was at the centre of the plot in the 1977 film *A Bridge Too Far*, filming was mainly carried out on a less developed bridge over the river in the nearby province of IJssel. Major General John Dutton Frost was born in India, but died very near my home in Chichester, West Sussex.

Holy Cross Bridge, Warsaw, Poland

Opened in 2000, the Holy Cross or Swietokrzyski Bridge crosses the Vistula River in central Warsaw. The cable-stayed road platform is 500 metres long and supported by twin vertical piers. The views from the bridge roadway of the national stadium and surrounding city are impressive at night, but I was unable to enjoy them, as when I crossed the bridge I was clinging on for dear life inside a Zuk fire engine headed at top speed to the nearby district of Praga.

River Bug Bridge, Brest, Belarus

A bridge connecting Warsaw to Terespol was first opened in the 1860s; at the time, both were within Russia. Several bridges have been built across the floodplain of the Bug and then destroyed before the one that stands here today, which serves as the current frontier between the European Union and the Commonwealth of Independent States. My experience of crossing the bridge on a dark winter night was very 'cold war'.

Bolshoy Kamenny Bridge, Moscow, Russian Federation

The current steel bridge crossing the Moskva river close to the Kremlin was completed in 1938, but there has been a crossing point near here since 1643. At over 105 metres long, today's bridge carries eight lanes of mainly stationary road traffic. The original stone bridge was lined with wooden shops and taverns. But today, other than cars there are only tourists on the bridge, as the best views of the Kremlin are to be had by using it to access the far bank of the river.

Novosibirsk Rail Bridge, Russian Federation

The current bridge across the River Ob was constructed in 2000 by adding stronger spans to the older granite piers, which date back to the 1890s. The bridge carries just a single rail track 980 metres across the river to the east of the city, known as the Chicago of Siberia, owing to its heavy industrialization. I found it virtually impossible to time any photographs of the view out the window of the train between the hundreds of metal girders.

Krasnoyarsk Bridge, Russian Federation

Crossing the massive river Yenisei, the original truss bridge was opened in 1899. Today there are actually three bridges across the river at this point. The road bridge, illustrated left, is very impressive, with five arches and a total length of 2,300 metres; at the time of its construction, it was the longest bridge in Russia. The rail bridge carries two tracks nearly a full kilometre between the banks of the river. When I crossed this bridge the train was met by mist and fog rising from the warmer river underneath; the river does not freeze here as it is close to one of the largest hydroelectric dams in the world.

Jade Belt Bridge, Beijing, China

Dating back to 1751, this marble bridge was built on Kunming Lake in the grounds of the Summer Palace. The single arch is significantly high to accommodate the dragon boat of the Qianlong Emperor. This style is also known as a 'moon bridge', the arch and its reflection in the water creating the circle symbolising the moon.

Gongchen Bridge, Hangzhou, China

The Grand Canal runs south for over 1,000 miles from Beijing as far as Hangzhou in Zhejiang Province. The Gongchen Bridge was constructed during the Ming Dynasty and has three arches and a hump back, a symbol of welcome and respect for the emperor. Marco Polo described Hangzhou as 'the city of heaven'. Were he a trainspotter, this would still be true, as the city is fully integrated into the high speed rail network.

Chengyang Bridge, Guangxi, China

This three-span covered bridge on the Linxi River was built in 1912 to connect two villages. Known as a 'wind and rain bridge', it got this name from the protection it offered people from poor weather. The bridge is made of wood, and no nails have been used, just dovetail joints. There are of course no trains to be found here; they pass nearby on the line to Guilin and south to Nanning.

Long Biên Bridge, Hanoi, Vietnam

Designed by Gustave Eiffel and built under French colonial rule in 1899, Long Biên is the oldest bridge in Hanoi. It was the first of several bridges crossing the Red River and connecting the inner suburbs of Hanoi to the centre. Although bombed during the American War, it continued to function. As a result, today it is seen as a symbol of pride to the people of Hanoi.

Japanese Bridge, Hoi An, Vietnam

The Japanese footbridge is located in the centre of the 16th-century trading port of Hoi An. It has a dual purpose, as it is also the temple of Tran Vo Bac De, the god of weather; sailors worshipped here to ensure safe passage on their trading routes. I had no bad weather experiences here, just a man who tried to charge me a 'tourist tax' to cross the bridge.

Dragon Bridge, Da Nang, Vietnam

Finished in 2012 at a reported cost of 1.5 trillion dong, the bridge was constructed to take on the form of a dragon in more ways than just its physical appearance. It is the only bridge that I have ever encountered that spews out fire and water to please the crowds each weekend evening. Over 650 metres long, it carries a six-lane highway from the city centre towards the outlying areas and the deserted coastal beach resorts.

French Bridge, Kampot, Cambodia

Kampot is an old French colonial town near the Gulf of Thailand in southern Cambodia. This old bridge has a unique design of several styles pushed into one structure. It was blown up during the Khmer Rouge period, but has been partially repaired and is still open to pedestrians and motorbikes today.

Bhumibol Bridge, Bangkok, Thailand

Opened in 2006, the Bhumibol Bridge, part of the city's southern ring road, crosses the Chao Phraya river. It is also known locally as the Mega Bridge, and you can see why from a long way away, as it has spiralling interchanges going up to the roadway 50 metres above the ground, suspended from two enormous pylons. There are actually two parallel bridges here, each with seven lanes of highway to cope with Bangkok's dreadful traffic. Far better to take the train, or a river boat!

River Kwae Bridge, Kanchanaburi, Thailand

The Bridge on the River Kwai actually used to cross the River Khwae Yai. Known as Bridge 277, it hasn't been moved, but the river it crosses was renamed after the success of the 1957 film of the same name (which was actually filmed in Sri Lanka). There were originally two railroad bridges over the river here, the one that stands today and a second, wooden, bridge upstream. Allied aircraft bombed both these bridges in 1945. The one that still stands today was repaired after the war with two Japanese-constructed central sections reconnecting the original curved spans.

Saphan Mon Bridge, Sangkhlaburi, Thailand

Close to the border to Myanmar, the Mon Bridge, or Saphan Mon, is the second longest wooden bridge in the world, at over 800 metres. Built by hand in the 1980s, it is something of a tourist landmark. Part of the bridge collapsed in 2013 as a result of weed growth and strong currents, but it has since been repaired and remains open to pedestrians.

Penang Bridge, Malaysia

Connecting mainland Malaysia with the island of Penang, this road bridge first opened in 1985. Its 8 kilometres across the busy Penang Strait gives drivers good views of the island from the roadway, suspended 33 metres above sea level so ships can pass freely underneath it. I chose to take the car ferry between Butterworth and Georgetown, a cheaper and faster solution in the local rush hour – and so I got good views of the bridge.

Cavenagh Bridge, Singapore

Built in 1870, and originally known as the Edinburgh Bridge, this structure was actually constructed in Glasgow and then shipped to Singapore where it was bolted and riveted together. Today it is a pedestrian-only bridge, but before the construction of the nearby Elgin Bridge, it was the only way to get cattle and rickshaws across the river in this part of the city. It's Singapore's oldest bridge still standing in its original form. I'm grateful it has been protected, as it provides me with a useful shortcut from my hotel to the nearby nightlife of Boat Quay.

Acknowledgements

I'm grateful to all those who helped make my second big train adventure happen.

Mark Hudson contributed the bridge illustration work for this book and also taught me all that I know on how to capture a bridge in a time of war. Colin Brooks designed the cover. Both are true gentleman of the advertising and design world. After the challenges of publishing *Trans-Siberian Adventures* I hadn't expected Caroline Petherick would still be my editor, so it's been great to have her as part of the team once more.

To Keith Parsons, for keeping me on the path of writing productivity and happiness. To Mark Smith, The Man in Seat 61, who continues to offer the best website in the world for planning a rail adventure. To the team at Real Russia – Igor, Yuriy, Doina, Tanya, Stacy and Natasha. To Alexey Samoylov, who taught me when to laugh like a Russian. To all my friends at my home in Chiang Mai for keeping me in such a great frame of mind whilst I was writing this book.

Finally, to all the wonderful people that I met on this journey who helped me along the way. It is these chance encounters and acts of kindness that makes solo rail travel so rewarding.

About the Author

Matthew Woodward is a rail-based adventurer and writer. He has completed several Trans-Siberian, Trans-Mongolian and Trans-Manchurian rail journeys from his home in Edinburgh, reaching destinations such as Shanghai, Singapore, Tokyo and Hong Kong by train. In 2016 he successfully completed a solo journey on the longest and highest railways in the world, to reach Lhasa by train.

He writes for a variety of media and publications on long-range train travel, and is a Fellow of the Royal Geographical Society and the Royal Asiatic Society. A self-confessed coffee addict, he carries an espresso machine wherever he travels. *A Bridge Even Further* is his second book.

If you enjoyed *A Bridge Even Further*, then you might like to also read Matthew Woodward's next book:

MATTHEW WOODWARD
THE RAILWAY TO HEAVEN

From the UK to Tibet on the longest and highest railways in the world

Chapter One:

The Man Who Would Be King

Tenzing strides ahead of me up the steep cobbled path towards the monastery. Looking upwards at him getting progressively further ahead, I feel frustrated not to be able to match his pace; my body is used to getting far more oxygen than is available in the thin air up here. I have to squint as I look upwards at him. The cloudless and saturated blue sky behind him is strangely ethereal. Despite the cold, the rising sun warms us, reflecting off the whitewashed buildings.

In many parts of the world I get introduced to people calling themselves Johnny (or its local equivalent), who obviously have a real name but choose to keep it secret. I guess they have found it's too hard for foreigners to pronounce or remember. But Tenzing really is called Tenzing, a popular name not just in Nepal[1] but

---

[1] Sherpa Tenzing was, with New Zealander Edmund Hillary, famous as being the first known to climb Everest and get back down successfully.

also here on the Tibetan Plateau. There is something about him that I put down to a military bearing and appearance, but I haven't asked him about his background. I suspect he has a particular set of skills that I hope won't be needed during our time together. Nonetheless it's reassuring to know that he's probably trained and prepared for any eventuality. Relaxed but confident, Tenzing is in many ways the perfect travel companion. His best asset is his smile. He smiles brightly when he speaks to anyone, and seems to have friends absolutely everywhere. He is proof that positive body language and politeness can get you just about anything you want.

Every few minutes he turns back to me and asks if I want to stop for a break, but I'm stubborn and determined to keep going. Unacclimatised to the altitude as I am, this small hill is proving a significant challenge to my feeble legs and lungs. Pilgrims and kids stride effortlessly past me, spinning huge brass prayer wheels as we make our way towards the entrance to the main courtyard. Spotting a bench on a rocky outcrop I have to stop – not only due to the urgent demands of my body, but also because I need time for my senses to take in the emerging scene in front of me.

Suntanned monks in their dark haematite-coloured robes are directing visitors as they enter the monastery. Pilgrims wave their arms in a mad fashion and whirl about at the bottom of the big stone steps. Some even crawl forwards on their bellies. Hypnotic sounds of bells ringing and Tibetan horns. Clouds of incense mixed with the scent of local flowers and juniper berries. Pinch myself hard. Have I arrived onto the film set of one of my favourite Kipling films, 'The Man Who Would be King'?

Once inside the outer walls, we walk together up the main path, where a long line of people, mainly women and children, are waiting. Many of the younger kids are crying and screaming, while the older ones just look miserable. This is very unusual in Tibet. Tenzing puts his smile on and leans over a little fence to speak to a monk at the entrance to the nondescript stone building. Not sure what to do, I stand at a respectable distance behind the line. Without explanation Tenzing returns and gestures for me to follow him through the crowd, whereupon another monk appears and opens a small side door that I hadn't noticed until then. The door is quickly shut behind us before the crowd notice us, leaving us alone and in the dark. As my eyes adjust, Tenzing explains that the monks here hold blessings for ill children in the afternoons. Our arrival has coincided with the Tibetan equivalent of a long wait at accident and emergency.

But we are not here for a blessing, and I don't yet know the purpose of our visit. I have a suspicion that we're now inside a building that we probably shouldn't be in. Around us lie dusty wooden cabinets and cupboards on a rough stone floor. Trickles of light penetrate through the cracks between the wooden planks of the heavy shutters covering the windows, and once Tenzing has found the switch, a solitary light bulb glows dimly above us.

I'm about to step forwards, but there is something unusual about the floor. Tenzing's arm holds me back and steadies me. I begin to make out strange shapes. In front of me on the ground is a complex painting made of many coloured sands: a mandala. It's about 3 metres square with incredible detail. The purpose of our visit here is for my introductory lesson from Tenzing in the symbolism of Tibetan Buddhism, and he explains to me how meditative monks have constructed this intricate design to represent the transient nature of material life. You have to concentrate hard and somehow imagine the shapes of the mandala inside yourself. The circles become a never-ending life, and proof that everything is connected. I stare at the pattern until I'm a bit cross-eyed and dizzy. Unused to the practice of meditation, I fail to reach enlightenment today. I shall have to return to complete my spiritual journey another time. With my first lesson over, I'm free to examine the objects in the cabinets nearby, while Tenzing goes into a passageway to look for the way through into the next room. It's strangely peaceful to be almost alone in here whilst still being able to hear the commotion outside.

When Tenzing returns he looks slightly concerned. This wouldn't mean anything to you unless you knew that normally his facial expression is one of beaming happiness, so even looking normal is a sign that something might be wrong. The trouble is that the doors in front of us and behind us are both locked shut. I have no fear, though. After all, I'm with a man who I suspect has been trained to break out of places more secure than this. He scans the room, tries a few other doors, and then jumps up to see if he can get to a little window. They are all securely locked. He pushes and adjusts the position of a couple of the cabinets, looking for a hidden doorway. I can't help but smile despite our circumstances. I'm back in one of my favourite childhood movies … all I need is a bull whip and the right hat. But dark thoughts cross my oxygen-starved mind. I hope Tenzing has a plan, otherwise a hundred years from now a monk might open the door and discover a couple of skeletons next to the mandala. Tenzing starts to bang on the little door, and I join in, as much for moral support as for the extra noise. But with the cacophony outside, no one can hear us.

Have you enjoyed this book?

If so, why not write a review on your favourite website?

If you would like to find out more about Matthew Woodward and his latest adventures, please visit:

www.matthew-woodward.com

You can also find him on Twitter at @OnTheRails and on Facebook at @LivingOnTheRails

Thank you for buying this Lanna Hall book.

Printed in Great Britain
by Amazon

71441568R00156